Mexico According to Eisenstein

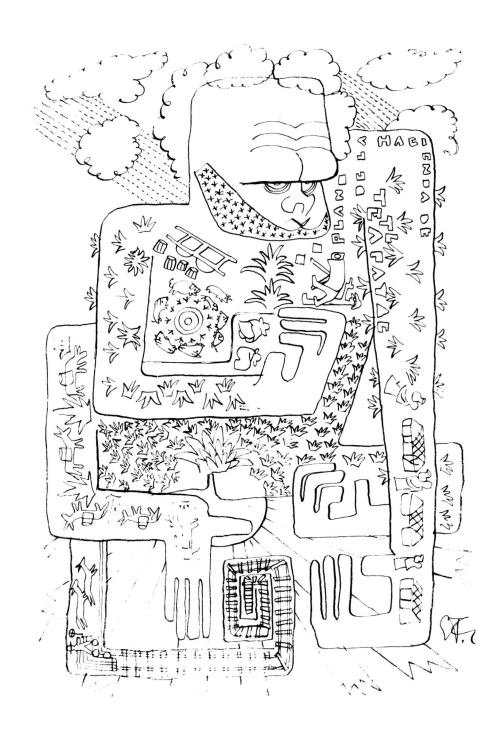

1. Gabriel Ledesma, Portrait of Eisenstein,
pen and ink, 1931.

MEXICO

ACCORDING TO

EISENSTEIN

Inga Karetnikova
in collaboration with Leon Steinmetz

University of New Mexico Press   *Albuquerque*

Library of Congress Cataloging in Publication Data

Karetnikova, Inga.
Mexico according to Eisenstein / Inga Karetnikova, in
collaboration with Leon Steinmetz. — 1st ed.
p.   cm.
Includes bibliographical references and index.
ISBN 0-8263-1256-X (cloth). — ISBN 0-8263-1257-8 (paper)
1. Eisenstein, Sergei, 1898–1948—Criticism and interpretation.
2. Que viva Mexico! (Motion picture)   3. Mexico in motion pictures.
4. Mexico—Description and travel.   5. Artists' preparatory studies.
I. Eisenstein, Sergei, 1898–1948.   II. Steinmetz, Leon.   III. Title.
PN1998.3.E34K37   1991
791.43'0233'092—dc20
90-23379
CIP

CONTENTS

ACKNOWLEDGMENTS

For permission to publish some of the pictorial material in this book and some of the reprints of Eisenstein's writings, grateful acknowledgment is due to the following museums, collections, and publishing houses: the Academy of Motion Picture Arts and Sciences, Beverly Hills; the British Film Institute, London; the Colegio de Pedro y Pablo, Mexico City; the Lilly Library, Indiana University, Bloomington; the Museum of Modern Art, Film Stills Archive, New York; the San Francisco Museum of Modern Art, Albert M. Bender Collection, San Francisco; Arno Press, New York (Sergei Eisentein, *Que Viva Mexico!,* 1972); Cambridge University Press, Cambridge (excerpts from Sergei Eisenstein, *Nonindifferent Nature,* translated by Herbert Marshall, 1987); Houghton Mifflin Company, Boston (excerpts from Sergei Eisenstein, *Immoral Memories: An Autobiography,* translated by Herbert Marshall, 1983); Indiana University Press, Bloomington, Indiana (excerpts from Harry Geduld and Ronald Gottesman, editors, *Sergei Eisenstein and Upton Sinclair: The Making and Unmaking of Que Viva Mexico!,* 1970); Iskusstvo, Moscow (excerpts from Sergei Eisenstein, *Selected Works in Six Volumes,* 1964); Princeton University Press, Princeton, New Jersey (Sergei Eisenstein, "The Prometheus of Mexican Printing," from *Film Essays and a Lecture,* edited by Jay Leyda, 1982).

I
FROM MOSCOW
TO TENOCHTITLAN

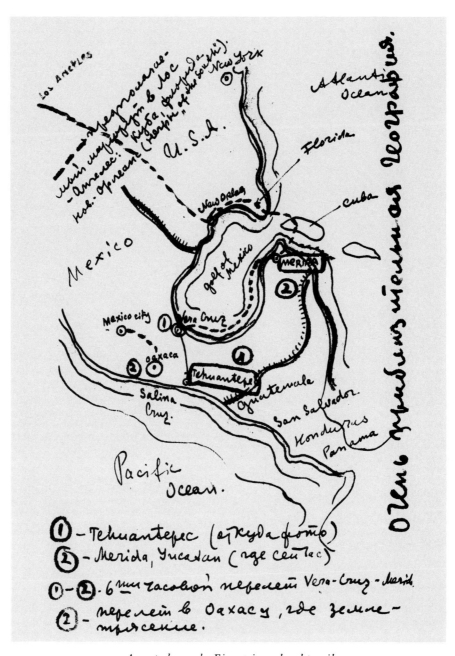

2. *A map drawn by Eisenstein, colored pencil.*

"We've been travelling up and down the whole map of Mexico. Pushkin himself {could have written} about us: 'they're washed by the rains, covered with dust.' The work is complicated, difficult, multi-lingual, but hellishly fascinating."[1]

Sergei Mikhailovich Eisenstein spent just over a year in Mexico—from December 1930 to February 1932. During this period he shot thousands of meters of his film *Que Viva Mexico!* and traveled hundreds of kilometers within the country. The filming was not yet completed when he had to halt the work. Stalin was demanding Eisenstein's return to Moscow: the director had long outstayed his leave of absence, and there was a rumor that he would prefer to remain abroad forever. In addition, the writer Upton Sinclair, who was subsidizing the production, cut off all funding. Eisenstein had overspent the budget and missed the contracted deadline.

In a letter to an American friend Eisenstein wrote:

> You know that instead of the four months' schedule and $25,000 which would have merely resulted in a pitiful travelogue we have worked thirteen months and have spent $53,000, but we have a great film and have expanded the original idea. This expansion was achieved under incredible difficulties inflicted upon us by the behavior and bad management of Upton Sinclair's brother-in-law, Hunter Kimbrough. . . . He presented me to Sinclair as a liar, blackmailer and God-knows-what else. My direct correspondence with Sinclair stopped. . . . The last part of my film, containing all the elements of a fifth act, is ruthlessly ripped out. . . I have exhausted my powers of persuasion. I shall do everything he wants. . . I accept everything, anything . . . if only they let me finish this film! . . . A film is not a sausage which tastes the same if you eat three-quarters of it or the whole

wurst. . . . You will hear horrible things about me (first, they are not true, and second, I know you don't care and I beg you to think only about the film). . . . Help us . . . No, not us, help our work, save it from mutilation!"[2]

But nothing could help Eisenstein. He and the crew, his cameraman Eduard Tisse, and his assistant Grigori Alexandrov, had to leave for Moscow, unable to complete *Que Viva Mexico!,* unable even to take with them the material they had already filmed. It remained with the Sinclairs. Later, the writer and his wife sold it in parts to various people and companies. An American producer, Sol Lester, edited the footage he bought into two films: *Thunder over Mexico* and *Death Day;* Pathé, the French company, made several ethnographic films from their share; the English journalist Marie Seton, (who was also Eisenstein's biographer), assembled the film *Time in the Sun.*[3] "Give up the hope of finding my film in the various screen versions of it emasculated by strangers' hands . . . ," wrote Eisenstein. "My whole conception has been destroyed; the sense of unity shattered; the efforts of many months annihilated by the absurd montage and the dispersion of the material. I shall try to get over that loss, the death of my creature, in which such love, effort and inspiration were placed."[4]

The film *Que Viva Mexico!* did not come to life, yet in his many shots for the film, in his script, in hundreds of drawings he did, in his writings about Mexico, composed at different times and in different places and scattered throughout his essays, letters, and memoirs, Eisenstein created an image of the country—both magnificent and unique.

In the life of Sergei Eisenstein, there was not one, but three Mexicos.

The first one was the *imaginary* Mexico of his youth; in 1921 in Moscow he had staged a Jack London story, *The Mexican,* and a few years later, he befriended Diego Rivera while the Mexican painter was visiting Soviet Russia. The second was the *real* Mexico he encountered in 1931 while shooting *Que Viva Mexico!* And finally, the third Mexico was the country of his *memory,* which remained with him until the end of his life. Even in the 1940s, while working on *Ivan the Terrible* and being entirely absorbed in the dramas of Russian history, Eisenstein would suddenly draw figures of peons or details of the Mexican landscape alongside his drawings of Russian churches and boyars. His attachment to the country would have seemed inexplicable if Eisenstein himself had not left some explanation for it: "During my encounter with Mexico, it seemed to me to be, in all the variety of its contradictions, a sort of outward projection of all those individual lines and features which I carried and carry within me like a tangle of complexes."[5]

The monumental simplicity of the old pyramids, the exuberant forms of the Mexican baroque, humble believers crawling uphill to the altars of the Madonna, the violent crowds surrounding the bullfight arenas, and the Carnivals of Death full of life, all attracted Eisenstein. He felt akin to Mexican contrasts and was able to comprehend their meaning, usually so inaccessible to foreigners.

Eisenstein's *imaginary* Mexico was composed of incidental impressions and random facts from history, politics, and literature, and from photographs and prints he saw by chance. Interestingly, though, his artistic career started with a Mexican topic. He was twenty-two years old, a recent student at the Petrograd Institute of Civil Engineering and a recent Red Army soldier, when he was asked to design sets and costumes for the play *The Mexican* at the Proletcult Theater in Moscow in October of 1920. Eisenstein, however, expanded his designer's duties and was actively involved in directing. In May of the following year *The Mexican* appeared on stage. Eisenstein wrote: "This is the plot: A Mexican revolutionary group needs money for its activities. A boy, a Mexican, offers to find the money. He trains for boxing, and contracts to let the champion beat him for a fraction of the prize. Instead he beats up the champion, winning the entire prize."[6]

The Mexican was staged within the new aesthetics of the avant-garde. The sets were made of cubes, cones, and spheres, and in some scenes even the actors looked like moving geometric figures. This play, with its denial of illusionistic settings and traditional costumes, was a step toward theatrical constructivism—the style which was soon to be summarized and formulated by the young Eisenstein's artistic mentor, Vsevolod Meyerhold.

Eisenstein didn't mean to bring to the play anything specifically Mexican, maybe just the *sombrero* because of its appealing "formalistic" shape—a circle combined with a cone. Yet, indirectly, he did recreate the Mexican atmosphere. In colors, especially in the sharp combination of yellow and blue, he expressed the intensity of the Mexican sunlight and the depth of the Mexican shadows. The colors were also intended to get a quick response from the audience, to "shock" them.

3. Eisenstein's stage design for the production of The Mexican, *watercolor, 1921.*

In the play the actors' faces were made up like masks. Only the protagonist, the Mexican, had an unmasked "real" face—he had to be distinguished, this "big patriot," as Jack London called him in his short story, the young man who "worked . . . hard for the coming Mexican revolution."[7]

Such zealous idealism was close to Eisenstein, just as it was to the entire generation of Soviet avant-garde of the early 1920s. They saw in the Bolshevik revolution a continuation, a carryover into life of the same innovative, rebellious impulse that inspired their artistic works. Thus Kazimir Malevich was convinced that the new, radical forms of his art foreshadowed the radical nature of the revolution. Vladimir Mayakovsky wrote: "To accept or not to accept? There was no such problem for me. . . . It was my revolution."[8] Marc Chagall used to say that Lenin turned Russia upside-down—exactly the way he did in his paintings. However, only a few years after the October Revolution it became obvious that avant-garde art was not wanted by the Soviet leaders. Lenin, especially, despised it, calling its masters "futurist scarecrows."

6

4. Eisenstein editing October, *1928. Courtesy of the British Film Institute.*

The new Soviet state wanted art that was realistic and openly propagandist. By the middle of the 1920s the period of the radical experimentation with methods, forms, and materials was over. Some of the avant-garde artists emigrated to Europe; some were forced to change their thinking; some were imprisoned; some committed suicide.

Eisenstein, however, was, for a while, in an exceptional position. Like his avant-garde fellow-artists, he was totally devoted to the ideas of "transforming the world," "building Communism," and "destroying the bourgoisie." His nonproletarian, upper-class background with all his German, French, and English governesses and tutors, music and dance teachers, with all the refined culture given to him purely by the fact of his birth, made him always feel guilty.[9] Perhaps, it even contributed to his fanaticism in both taking up the cause of the revolution and using the revolution as the sole theme of his early films.

Owing to the unprecedented worldwide success and political influence of his film *The Battleship Potemkin* (1925), he was at first forgiven almost any cinematic experiments, especially since he always knew how to make the most formalistic device enhance the propagandistic force of his work.[10] But in 1927–28, the party critics began their attacks on him, and declared his new film *October* "a conspicuous failure of experimental cinema" completely incomprehensible to "the masses."

Around this time, in November of 1927, Eisenstein met Diego Rivera, who came to Moscow for the tenth anniversary of the revolution. The highly regarded Mexican painter had been wanting to visit the Soviet Union for a long time. He liked to emphasize that it was the impact of the Russian upheaval of 1917 that brought him out of bohemian Paris and impelled him to create murals for the people of Mexico. Now he was commissioned by the Soviet government to paint murals on the walls of the Red Army Club; furthermore, the general secretary of the Communist party, Joseph Stalin, expressed a wish to pose for a portrait by Rivera. ". . . The campaign for the apotheosis of Stalin had begun, and his face appeared simultaneously on the cover of every paper and magazine in the country, while every prominent artist was set to doing his bust or portrait. It was this campaign to which Diego unwittingly contributed."[11] (But if Rivera contributed to the cult of Stalin at its very beginning, then Eisenstein, almost two decades later, would give to this cult a more sophisticated treatment. In his film *Ivan the Terrible, Part One,* he would justify all of the dreaded czar's actions and, in a very subtle way, associate Ivan with Stalin.)

When Eisenstein first met Rivera at one of the artist's presentations in Moscow, he was prepared for this meeting by Mayakovsky's stories about Rivera and Mexico and by his poems about that country.[12] The poet had traveled to Mexico in 1925 and was Rivera's guest there. Later he wrote: "Diego Rivera met me at the railway station. . . . The only thing I had heard about him before was that he was the greatest Mexican painter, and that with a bullet from his Colt he could hit a coin thrown in the air. . . . He turned out to be quite an imposing fellow, with a big belly and a wide, ever smiling face. He tells thousands of interesting stories, throwing Russian words into his speech (Diego understands Russian perfectly) . . ."[13]

That evening in Moscow Rivera spoke about art in the service of the world revolution, and specifically about Mexican monumental painting, which he considered both the result and the continuation of the Mexican revolution. Rivera wanted to convince everybody that the frescoes he and his Mexican colleagues were painting on the walls of the public buildings were the only art form accessible to the masses. After all, his Soviet comrades, not long ago, also were happy to proclaim: "The streets are our brushes; our palettes—the city squares!"[14] Forgetting his past as one of the most successful cubists in Paris, forgetting his many easel paintings, Rivera now condemned easel painting as a "desolate bourgeois form."

This political jargon and Rivera's categorical stance were familiar to Eisenstein: after all, Rivera was a Marxist and a member of the Communist party. But at the same time, he expressed considerable independence in his ideology, which to the Soviet artists, including Eisenstein, was rather striking. Rivera, on the other hand, couldn't quite comprehend their status as government workers and couldn't understand their total surrender of their independence. His political opinions were expressions of his freedom of choice, to some extent an artistic pose, occasionally even a game. For instance, when Rivera, then the general secretary of the Mexican Communist party, was temporarily expelled from the party in 1929, he

> arrived, sat down, and took out a large pistol and put it on a table. He then put a handkerchief over the pistol, and said: "I, Diego Rivera, general secretary of the Mexican Communist party, accuse the painter Diego Rivera of collaborating with the petit-bourgeois government of Mexico and of having accepted a commission to paint the stairway of the National Palace of Mexico. This contradicts the politics of the Comintern and therefore the painter Diego Rivera should be expelled from the Communist party by the general secretary of the Communist party, Diego Rivera." Diego declared himself expelled, and he stood up, removed the handkerchief, picked up the pistol, and broke it. It was made of clay.[15]

Rivera told Eisenstein that he had seen *The Battleship Potemkin* and that the film was close to monumental painting—the highest compliment he could have paid. By the time he visited Moscow, Rivera had already completed his murals in Mexico's Ministry of Education—over a hundred frescoes on Mexican life and the Mexican past, painted in his clear, firm style. Rivera spoke obsessively of the Mexican artistic heritage, of the ancient Aztec capital Tenochtitlan, of the pyramids, temples, and palaces of the Aztecs and the Mayans, and of their sculpture and painting. He insisted that the traditions of ancient Mexican art, its symbolism and mythology, were no less important to contemporary Mexican culture than classic Greek art was to the European Renaissance. He believed that Soviet painters were making a mistake in denying the Russian artistic heritage—the icon painting—this "real cultural treasure."

For Soviet ideologues this statement sounded almost like a call to return to the "religious prejudices" of prerevolutionary time. They also disliked Rivera's criticism of easel painting; in Soviet art it had already become an established and flexible form for Communist propaganda.

During Rivera's stay in the Soviet Union the official attitude toward him changed dramatically. This was mutual; his feelings toward Soviet Russia changed as well. The Moscow of 1927 turned out to be different from what he had imagined. He would speak of this after his return to Mexico, would condemn Stalinism, and for a while would become an ardent follower of Leon Trotsky. (He would even give Trotsky and his wife refuge in his home in Coyoacan.)

Rivera spent six months in Moscow, and he had not even started working on the murals for the Red Army Club. His patrons continually postponed his work. In May of 1928 he suddenly left for Mexico without saying goodbye to Eisenstein or to his other Russian friends. But Eisenstein and Rivera would meet again, four years later, in Mexico. "The seed of interest in that country . . . nourished by the stories of Diego Rivera, when he visited the Soviet Union . . . grew into a burning desire to travel there," wrote Eisenstein.[16]

In December of 1930 Eisenstein, his cameraman Tisse, and his assistant Alexandrov arrived in Mexico. It had been almost two years since they left the Soviet Union for a working tour of Germany, Switzerland, France, England, and the United States. Eisenstein spent half a year in Hollywood developing several film projects for Paramount, among them—a full-length screen adaptation of Theodore Dreiser's *An American Tragedy*. Although Hollywood's David O. Selznick admitted that it was the most moving script he had ever read, he rejected it as too expensive to produce. He said, "as entertainment, I don't think it has one chance in a hundred."[17] Two other scripts of Eisenstein, *The Glass House* and *Sutter's Gold,* were also rejected by Paramount. Ivor Montagu, Eisenstein's English friend who collaborated with him on the scripts for Hollywood, wrote: ". . . mistrust of intellectuals, . . . tribal rivalry within the . . . company [Paramount], our own tactical mistakes, and political fears [:] It cannot be known which defeated us, which—if any—would not have been decisive without the others."[18]

So Eisenstein's relationship with Paramount did not work out and now it was time for him and his crew to return to Moscow—their leave of absence was almost over. But Eisenstein had an urge which he just could not set aside—to visit Mexico and to make a film about that country.

It was Charlie Chaplin who suggested a sponsor for the film—Upton Sinclair, a radical writer "who had a record of vigorously supporting the Revolution and was one of the most widely read and deeply respected foreigners in the Soviet Union."[19]

A contract was written and signed.[20] Neither Eisenstein, who had never handled any financial aspects of filmmaking, nor Sinclair and his wife Mary, who later on would not even be able to comprehend why Eisenstein would need so many retakes, nor Sinclair's brother-in-law, Hunter Kimbrough, a stock and bond salesman, who without the slightest experience became the general business manager of the film, had any idea of the sum of money that would be needed for the production, film stocks, and travel across Mexico. Eisenstein named a random figure—$25,000—and announced that he personally wanted no salary: all he needed was a dollar a day to feed himself, Tisse and Alexandrov.[21] The period of shooting was set in the contract as three or four months.

They arrived in Mexico City on December 9, 1930, and in four days they started filming some documentary scenes of the Fiesta of the Virgin of Guadalupe and the bullfights, the corridas, which were taking place simultaneously.

Eisenstein was very happy with the start. Mary Sinclair found him "an extremely fine type of person, very much wrapped up in his art,"[22] and Upton Sinclair told his friends that this was the first time in Eisenstein's life that he was entirely free to make a picture according to his own ideas.

However there were some rather unpleasant incidents also. A few weeks after their arrival, Eisenstein and his crew, including Hunter Kimbrough, were, for no reason at all, arrested by the Mexican police, who wanted to know the "purpose" of this Russian-American expedition. They were released shortly, however, and issued an apology and a permit to shoot the film anywhere in the country; a few weeks later the Mexican president invited the crew to visit him in Acapulco.

On January 14, 1931, Hunter Kimbrough sent a telegram to Sinclair: "Eisenstein and boys leaving immediately aeroplane for Oaxaca . . . earthquake . . . ," and on January 22 Eisenstein and Tisse's film *The Earthquake in Oaxaca* was shown in Mexico City.[23] The local newspaper called it "the most authentic report about the terrible national disaster." The film, the only documentary ever made by Eisenstein, has not survived. But from a list of the film's captions, published recently in a book about Eisenstein,[24] one can visualize some of the shots: "the river that flowed past the city has changed its course" . . . "the streets are filled with people" . . . "half the city has been destroyed within a few minutes" . . . "the volcano's eruption ruined cathedrals, the houses of the rich, the houses of the poor . . . and the homes of the dead" (the earthquake had dislodged corpses from their graves). The list of captions ends with the words, "These people have lost everything. Their misfortune demands your compassion."

In his memoirs Eisenstein mentioned only his flight to Oaxaca without describing the disaster:

> Popocatepetl is so real that once we nearly crashed into its crater in the tiny plane that carried us to the borders of Guatemala to film a catastrophe resulting from one of the earthquakes so frequent in Mexico.
> Curiosity drove us to peer into the extinct crater of the mysterious Popo.
> Not checking the contents of our fuel tank, we made an aerial detour up and around.
> You should have seen the deadly white faces of the navigator and pilot as, with a choking motor, they whirled us, "gliding," toward the outskirts of Mexico City, just missing the tops of the telephone poles![25]

Eisenstein's film was to be called *Que Viva Mexico!* This was the only thing that he knew for sure. So far he was simply getting accustomed to Mexico, becoming acquainted with the people, architecture, and art. He was spending many hours in the renowned National Archaeological Museum, studying what was left of Indian civilization. He also wanted to seek out all that remained of Tenochtitlan, the Aztec capital, on whose foundations Mexico City had been built. Very helpful to him was the recently published book *Idols Behind Altars*. Its author, Anita Brenner, was Diego Rivera's friend, and it was probably Rivera who gave the book to Eisenstein. Using as her main source Spanish chronicles of the sixteenth century (the "documentary genre" of that time), Brenner wrote about the Indians and the Spanish conquest. She wrote about Mexican traditions and beliefs, about miracles, and about art and artists, starting with the painters who were sent by the last Aztec king, Montezuma, to Hernando Cortes. They were commissioned to draw on cotton cloths the Spaniards, their ships, their horses, and "everything else in sight."[26] Eisenstein was fascinated by Brenner's view of Mexican culture as accepting the Spanish traditions but also preserving the past, hiding the Indian idols behind the Catholic altars.

Rivera took the time to show Eisenstein the frescoes in the National Palace, which depicted scenes from Mexican history. Rivera also invited him to his home, the Blue House, in Coyoacan. A photograph taken in the garden shows Eisenstein with Rivera and his twenty-four-year-old wife, the "beautiful and clever" Frida Kahlo. The paintings that made her known as one of Mexico's most original artists hadn't yet been created, although her style ("agonized poetry," as Rivera described it, or "a ribbon around a bomb," according to André Breton), was already formed. Eisenstein saw her candid pictures made in the Mexican folk tradition on sheets of tin. They were only about herself, her inner life, and her dreams—such a refreshing shock for the Soviet film director who, prior to that time, used to think in terms of *typages*[27] and social classes. Frida and Diego's home, with its remarkable collection of folk and ancient art, was invaluable to Eisenstein's discovery of Mexico.

Rivera took Eisenstein to Cuernavaca, some fifty miles from Mexico City. There, in the Cortes Palace, which Mexico's conqueror had built for himself, Rivera had painted frescoes of the conquest. Eisenstein was captivated by the murals: passing from one fresco to another, he, as a viewer, brought the element of movement into immobile images. In his world of the cinema everything was exactly the opposite—the film moved while the viewer was immobile. Eisenstein liked this gradual unraveling of Rivera's visual narrative from one historical episode to the next. His own montage usually shattered the continuity of narration; Eisenstein strove to establish the "sign" of an event, rather than retell it. In this sense, the method of another Mexican painter, Rivera's contemporary, José Clemente Orozco, was closer to that of the director. Orozco concentrated on the condensed symbolic image rather than on the story. Overall, Eisenstein considered Orozco the most passionate among the Mexican mural painters—he called him Prometheus—and he deeply regretted that he was unable to meet him personally. He did however meet a few months later, in Taxco, the third famous Mexican mural painter, David Alfaro Siqueiros.

During the earliest days of Eisenstein's stay in Mexico City, he saw only some of Siqueiros's works, among them the fresco *Burial of a Worker*. It was

5. *Frida Kahlo*, Frida and Diego Rivera, *oil on canvas, 39 x 31 ½, 1931.*
Courtesy of the San Francisco Museum of Modern Art, Albert M. Bender Collection.

14

unfinished because of some political scandal, but even in this incomplete state its composition impressed him: a close-up of the workers' faces, resembling Aztec masks, and "a coffin of intense aquamarine . . . a paroxysm of despair. . . ."[28]

Eisenstein made friends with Jean Charlot, a skillful painter and a keen art historian, and also with Roberto Montenegro, who some time later painted a portrait of Eisenstein on the wall of Peter and Paul College in Mexico City. The director is dressed as a Spanish conquistador, with a strip of film in his hands.

So far everything was going well. Moscow's attitude toward Eisenstein's Mexican project was favorable. Sinclair agreed that *Que Viva Mexico!* should not be just an entertaining travelogue. Leopold Stokowsky offered to conduct the music for the film. Both Mexican and American newspapers expressed a steady interest in the work. Even Hunter Kimbrough was satisfied and informed the Sinclairs that the biggest Mexican newspaper gave Eisenstein a "front-page write up" and put in a large picture of the Russian director.

At the end of January, before leaving for Tehuantepec, an old southern town, Eisenstein completed the first short and sketchy script for the film.

There is a map of one of his trips, drawn by him and bearing some of his notes. Circled in red are the cities of Tehuantepec and Merida—the first major stops along the route.

For two months in Tehuantepec Eisenstein and his crew filmed the primeval, sensuous life of tropical Mexico. In one of his letters Eisenstein wrote that Eden was located not between the Tigris and the Euphrates, but rather somewhere between the Gulf of Mexico and Tehuantepec. They filmed the everyday life of the people, the fiestas with their elaborate costumes, a wedding ceremony, markets. Eisenstein, who all his life had been a passionate student of history, was delighted to find himself literally transplanted into a matriarchal society, with its simple lifestyle and primitive trade. Much later, in his memoirs, he recalled some of his observations of Tehuantepec:

> In desolate tropical villages I sit with a circle of women who are sorting out, with mysterious murmurings, numberless little dishes made from little local pumpkins. Pinch after pinch of ground black coffee slips into those dishes from hand to hand. They are echoed by a counterflow, in definite proportion, of some kind of locally grown bean—all in the same kind of

little dishes. The clang of the little dishes against each other creates the characteristic murmur of this scene, which is otherwise conducted in total silence.[29]

The women of Tehuantepec, the Tehuanas, willingly posed for the camera, and sometimes in small villages they were, as in their natural state, almost completely nude.

Up until that time Eisenstein, along with Soviet art in general, shunned the themes of the human body and sex as decadent and bourgeois, morally weakening, distracting from the class struggle. But here, in this easy, tropical atmosphere, these beliefs had no meaning. For the first time in his creative life Eisenstein was working with images free from any social, political, or religious conflicts, and he enjoyed it.

In the very beginning of March the party left Tehuantepec for Merida, a city in Yucatan which, unlike the Indian Tehuantepec, had a strong Spanish influence in its architecture and customs. There Eisenstein filmed churches and religious services, and, often in the same day, corridas, which appeared to him no less ritualistic than the Christian ceremonies. He even saw a relation between the two. He later wrote: "During the same Sunday celebrations the blood of Christ from the morning Mass in the cathedral is mixed with the torrents of bull's blood of the afternoon bullfight in the . . . arena."[30]

The hero of the season was an eighteen-year-old matador, David Liceaga. Hundreds of shots were made of his fights in the arena. For close-ups of his footwork and cape work, Liceaga posed for the camera separately. Also posing for close-ups were the bullfight queens—the prettiest girls of Merida. The waving of their fans was part of the corrida's rhythm.

Eisenstein filmed corridas again and again. Ignoring Kimbrough's lamentations about spending time and throwing money away, he was utterly absorbed in his search for the expressive images of the corrida, of its unity of "danger and style." Three decades later, the celebrated Mexican poet Octavio Paz would say what it seems Eisenstein wanted to reveal about the artistic aspect of the corrida: "The bullfighter strictly complies with a form at the risk of his life. It is what we call *temple* in Spanish: a cool boldness, a well-tempered musical harmony, stubborn courage and flexibility."[31]

There was also something else at that time that made Eisenstein happy. "I began to draw, . . . a paradise lost and found," he wrote.[32]

He had a natural gift for drawing and drew brilliantly from his early childhood. But his film career developed so suddenly and forcefully that the artist had to step aside for the film director, handing over to him the ability to think in visual terms. He stopped drawing. This interruption lasted almost nine years, until he came to Mexico. Whereas before it had been the draftsman who handed his experience over to the filmmaker, now the filmmaker returned the favor to the draftsman.

Film increased his sensitivity to rhythm. The unreeling of the film, in a way, pushed him toward the idea of graphic series, where the connection between the sheets of drawings is similar to the connection between shots in a film sequence. And because of the cinema's closeness to "real" forms, he appreciated even more the fragile quality of free line, that illusion which does not exist in nature. "In Mexico, . . . I once again began to draw. And now in the correct linear style. The influence here was not so much Diego Rivera, who drew with thick, broken strokes, but rather the pure 'mathematical' line, so dear to my heart."[33]

His Mexican drawings are something of "visual notes" on his work—the flow of the mind from one image to another while he was structuring *Que Viva Mexico!* He drew "very quickly so as not to disturb the subconscious elements."[34]

The drawings were made with ordinary pencil on scraps of paper— sometimes with a hotel letterhead. Eisenstein never anticipated that the public would see them. Accustomed as he was to addressing his work to millions, his drawings he left for himself.[35]

Eisenstein's austere line does not convey a realistic representation, but rather the graphic symbols of faces, figures, or "traces of movement." In a way, his drawings echo Mexican pictographs where the form of the object or figure is transformed into an ornamental symbol. Just as in pictographs, the representation in his drawings is freed from all accidental details. The artist always conforms to the classical formula: drawing at its best is the art of omitting and synthesizing a great many lifelike elements in order to create a symbol and to express an idea. Even the sketches he made from real life, right on the spot—a procession of water-bearers, worshippers of the Madonna, faces and figures of Indians from Yucatan, priests from Merida—all are engraved in an unadorned, uninterrupted line, which, racing over the paper, eliminates all that is an obstacle to generalization.

The grotesque and the epic are two primary aspects of Eisenstein's Mexican drawings; Mexico's own sharp contrasts prompted this. Being very receptive and open to all impressions, Eisenstein assimilated material not only from ancient and modern Mexican art, but from its folk art, from primitive toys, even from painted household wares. "These primitives. For fourteen months I avidly explored them with my hands and eyes."[36]

The whole month of April they spent in Yucatan, in the ancient Mayan capital of Chichen Itza which means "City of the Sacred Well." In a letter written at that time, Sinclair described the shots of *Que Viva Mexico!* as "gorgeous beyond all telling." Throughout all this time, Eisenstein never saw any of the material he had filmed; it was all sent to Hollywood for developing and remained with Sinclair, who regularly invited guests and the press for viewings. In the same letter Sinclair wrote that after seeing the pieces filmed in Tehuantepec, the "Mexican Vice Consul said: 'These pictures will be a revelation even to the Mexicans.'"[37] In a letter to Eisenstein sent from California to Mexico Sinclair complained that he still hadn't seen the script and had no idea how the magnificent shots and episodes would relate to each other. Eisenstein was not in a hurry to reveal all of his intentions to Sinclair. The director was against making a romantic Mexican story, commercially secure, something that Sinclair would be happy with.

Eisenstein wanted to turn Mexico itself into the plot of the film. Only now, after being here for almost six months, did he start to understand the country. He called it his spiritual homeland and, even before leaving Mexico, already missed it.

> You climb the thousand-year-old pyramids of Yucatan and sit purposely
> at the base of the ruined Temple of a Thousand Columns in order to gaze at
> the familiar outline of the Great Bear, lying upside down in the Mexican
> sky, and wait for the moment it sinks behind the Pyramid of Warriors. And
> how you sit there deliberately trying to fix the memory of this moment in
> the future stream of recollections, much as seamen fix their course by the
> very same stars.[38]

In Chichen Itza, amidst "the immobile eternity of stone" and in "the shadow of the ruins," Eisenstein and his crew filmed an old Mayan funeral ceremony. Here Eisenstein made some shots that have now become classics, in which the stone faces of Mayan sculptures and the faces of modern-day Mexicans are captured together in one shot, in one frame, at the same angle, revealing the amazing similarity in their features. Eisenstein could not refrain from having his own picture taken in a shot with the very same composition—his profile and the profile of a Mayan sculpture.

He returned from Merida to Mexico City by boat at the end of April and in early May moved onto the hacienda Tetlapayac, located among the enormous maguey plantations of central Mexico.

By that time the script for *Que Viva Mexico!* was completed. It had a finished, literary form, but no specific details yet. "What the script gives us is not the finished film, shot by shot, but merely the ground plan, a plan which might be varied . . . as the work went on," wrote Leon Moussinac in his book about Eisenstein.[39] Eisenstein believed that a screenplay serves mainly as a source of inspiration for the director. To his mind, shooting should freely interpret the script just as editing (or, to use his favorite word, *montage*), in turn, interprets the filmed material. In his work on the script of *Que Viva Mexico!* he was inspired, as he used to say, by the "montage" of the country itself, where movement through space, from one province to another, is also a voyage through centuries of time. Eisenstein was amazed that in Mexico the sequence of epochs was presented not "vertically (in years and centuries), but horizontally, as the geographic coexistence of the most diverse stages of culture."[40] Thus, not far from the still matriarchal Tehuantepec lay plantations and lands with feudal customs, like the hacienda Tetlapayac, and next to that was twentieth-century Mexico City. Eisenstein compared the country to a serape, the traditional striped garment: Mexico was similarly striped, with "violently contrasting" cultures existing side by side and at the same time centuries apart.

According to the script, the film would consist of a prologue, four episodes (he called them "novellas")—*Sandunga, Maguey, Fiesta,* and *Soldadera,* and an epilogue. Each novella would be different in its material (the primitive Mexico, the Catholic, the revolutionary, and the modern) and in its mood, and still the whole would be held together by a free poetic composition, and every part would be a variation on the theme of birth and death.

Eisenstein discovered that in Mexico, as nowhere else, life and death cross each other's path "in the tragic images of death stamping out life, or in the sumptuous images of the triumph of life over death. . . . At every step one sees birth mingled with death, in the immutable vision of a cradle in every sarcophagus, in the rosary at the top of the crumbling pyramid and in the fateful, half-erased words on a sculpted skull: 'I was like you, you shall be like me, . . .'"[41] Eisenstein learned that in ancient Mexico the unity of life and death was personified in the Aztec goddess Coatlicue, who seized man in death and yet, at the same time, gave people their lives. The author of *The Battleship Potemkin* planned in his Mexican film to turn Coatlicue into a new historical symbol by bringing a third element to her birth-death duality— the theme of *rebirth* of the Indian culture.

Thus, he wanted to place the ancient funeral ritual in Yucatan in the prologue of *Que Viva Mexico!* "for purely symbolic purposes . . . to represent the death of ancient cultures before the coming of new times."[42] In the prologue, the relatives of the deceased sitting motionless around the open coffin, are as immobile as the corpse. In contrast, the epilogue was to be all action—the Mexican carnival celebration of the Day of the Dead, wild and joyful, with dancing skeletons. In the prologue Eisenstein would show man's resignation to destruction, and in the epilogue his sarcasm toward it. In the prologue there is individual, "biological" death; the epilogue asserts the immortality of the nation.

Between the prologue and the epilogue, the film was to depict "the peon who is trampled to death by the hoofs of the hacendado's horse, and the Catholic monk who in a blasphemous renunciation of both himself and the ascetic rule, stamps out the lush celebration of tropical life and the bull who loses his blood in the arena to the glory of the Virgin Mary, and the country itself which is also bleeding to death, torn apart as it is by fratricidal civil conflicts. . . ."[43]

The material for the first novella, *Sandunga,* about the tropical, primitive Tehuantepec, had already been filmed. At the hacienda Tetlapayac, located on Mexico's central plateau, Eisenstein filmed the second novella, *Maguey.* Tetlapayac was "a lonely, beautiful and haunting building; changeless, yet changing with every movement of the sun . . . an old Spanish plantation belonging to Don Julio Saldivar . . . a fortress with coral pink walls . . . and two high towers like sentinels rising above a sea of symmetrical, immobile, grey-green cactus—the maguey. . . ."[44] From the thick white "blood" of the maguey, the Mexicans make pulque, the national drink.

The second novella of *Que Viva Mexico!* tells of the time of the dictatorship of Porfirio Diaz, before the 1910 Revolution. Sebastian, a young Indian who works on the maguey plantations, wants to marry a girl named Maria, and, according to custom, he goes to his hacendado for his permission and blessing. The role of Sebastian was played by a real peon from the maguey plantation; Maria—by a painter, Isabel Villasenor; and the hacendado was played by the real hacendado Saldivar, whose ancestors owned Tetlapayac and the huge maguey plantations—the authentic sets for *Maguey*. Eisenstein wrote: "Customs on the haciendas are feudal. The hacienda is a former monastery. The tall gates are closed in the evening, and none of the management choose to go outside at night."[45]

One of the drunken guests of the hacendado kidnaps Maria and rapes her. Sebastian and his friends get some ammunition and a gunfight breaks out. Eisenstein wrote: "For many days in a row we have been filming in an undergrowth of shaggy cactuses, or amid the sparse leaves of maguey, various episodes of the skirmish between the insurgent peons and the landlord's militia—the charros—in narrow striped pants, monumental spurs, and felt hats trimmed with gold braid. The performance is unusually realistic. In fact, the actors are real peons and actual charros from the *oprichnina*[46] of young señor Julio."[47] Sebastian and two other peons are captured and buried in the ground up to their necks, then their heads are trampled by galloping horses.

Maguey was dedicated to Diego Rivera. For Eisenstein the theme of the peons—their struggle, their everyday life and appearance, their work at the cactus plantations—all were intimately associated with Rivera's frescoes. Eisenstein even compared Rivera himself with the nopal cactus, that grows in a variety of curves, which can be sharp and prickly like Rivera in his satirical paintings. "Diego can bloom as well—just as the sharp [thorns] of the nopal, with pink, yellow, blue, and white buds, equal the sweet Sandunga or the flower fiesta of Xochimilco."[48]

The Sinclairs showed the pieces of *Maguey* to representatives of the international press. Reactions were enthusiastic. Although Eisenstein was strongly opposed to showing this unorganized, unedited material to anyone, the Sinclairs had the final say. Gradually their relations with Eisenstein worsened—first because of his overspending, although expenditures were quite frugal; then because the scheduled timetable was not adhered to. Often delays were not the director's fault; at times it would rain for weeks, and a cameraman was seriously ill. From time to time Sinclair would suggest something absolutely unthinkable to Eisenstein; for instance, he wanted *Maguey* to be completed as a separate film, as a "real story" in the Hollywood sense which could be "sold at once"—an idea that appalled Eisenstein. An additional source of constant conflict was the manager, Hunter Kimbrough, who couldn't comprehend either the nature of filmmaking, or the peculiarities of the filmmaker. How severe the problem became is evident from the letter Kimbrough wrote to Sinclair from hacienda Tetlapayac:

> I am a little rough with him [Eisenstein] these days. I am cutting down on his pocket money and fuss when they eat too much. I let him run his own errands and talk pretty rough to him at times. He's like a Negro. Kind words and consideration are not enough. It is just over his head. But he is quite all right and will remain so if you'll let him know I'm in charge and what I say is final. . . .[49]

Most significant, though, was the change of attitude toward Eisenstein in Moscow. In November 1931 Stalin sent Sinclair the following telegram: "Eisenstein loose [*sic*] his comrades' confidence in the Soviet Union. He is thought to be deserter who broke off with his own country . . . I am afraid the people here would have no interest in him soon. . . ."[50] Stalin could not abide independence in Soviet citizens, even those as exceptional as Eisenstein. What's more, one of the fiercest opponents of Eisenstein's "formalistic" art became the head of the Soviet film industry; insidiously he did all he could to subject Eisenstein's films and his film theory to negative criticism, to bring Eisenstein "into line," and to ensure that the director would return from Mexico a failure. Times had become still harder. Soviet propaganda, in the unifying language of socialist realism, was now obligatory for every Soviet artist and writer. The material of *Que Viva Mexico!* was neither useful nor appropriate for the Communist party; it was therefore not needed in Moscow. Sinclair sensed this and probably drew his conclusions.

Eisenstein did not know exactly what was going on behind his back, but he could guess most of it. However, the troubles in Mexico and the anxiety over what awaited him in Moscow could not slow the intensity of his work. He, Tisse, Alexandrov, and some of his Mexican assistants traveled frequently from Tetlapayac for some additional shots or documentary scenes to

Acapulco, or to the rich and dynamic Puebla, with its famous cathedrals, services, and corridas.

They filmed fragments for different parts of the film at once, depending on the weather, the light, and the events that took place.

They were filming a fiesta "in dusty Taxco, under a burning sun [where] the same natives had not changed for hundreds and hundreds of years."[51] There Eisenstein met David Alfaro Siqueiros and dedicated the prologue of *Que Viva Mexico!* to him, in honor of his fresco *Burial of a Worker.* The director had been influenced by this work. Later, Eisenstein's montage—the juxtaposition and collision of visual images—would in turn become a major influence in Siqueiros's art.[52] In February 1932, just prior to Eisenstein's departure from Mexico, he helped to organize an exhibition of Siqueiros's painting and spoke at the opening.

In Taxco Eisenstein filmed the Day of the True Cross, a fragment for his third novella, called *Fiesta* (or *Spanish Milagro*) which was to show the Spanish social and religious influence in Mexico. He continued filming the similar religious celebration in Mexico City: the pilgrims who crawled on their knees in ecstasy for miles to the Hill of Tepeyac, on which stands the shrine of the "Dark Madonna," patroness of the nation and protectress of the humble; and people praying and dancing in the church to the sounds of drums and flutes.

> The dance is intoxicating in its unchanging melody. The cries of the pilgrims' children rend the air. The mothers thrust out their breasts for them. The organ sounds. The candles burn. Heat and intoxication. And the endless flow of human figures, pouring with sweat, crawl on their knees from the base of the pyramid to its holy heights. Knees are wrapped in rags. Sometimes in cushions that get torn to shreds. Often on their heads are fantastic headdresses of feathers. . . .[53]

Eisenstein wondered if perhaps the entire celebration was also in honor of an ancient Aztec goddess, Tonantzin; her temple once stood where the Lady of Guadalupe's shrine is now. "The Catholics . . . raised churches in exactly the same places, on the peaks of . . . pyramids, in order not to sidetrack the pilgrims, who for thousands of years had come from all the corners of the land to the foot of these very pyramids."[54]

The other material for this novella included an acted scene of three pilgrims carrying cactuses bound in cross form to their outspread arms and scenes of Mexico's subjugation by the conquistadors filmed in the rhythm of ritual dances. But the main theme of *Fiesta* was the corrida.

The filming of this novella remained unfinished. The script sets forth its plot only very generally, and in his letters Eisenstein purposefully tried to be vague on this subject, so as not to transgress the religious sentiments of Catholic Mexico. Only Eisenstein's surviving drawings of the corrida allow any insight into his intentions.

There are numerous drawings on this theme and hundreds of meters of film devoted to it. Fragments of film show the ceremony of the dressing of the matador, David Liceaga; his veneration of the Madonna before his performance; the benediction of the torrero by his mother; the solemn entrance into the arena; the subtleties of the play of banderillas; the masterful interweaving of steps in the confrontation with the bull. In the drawings only the main heroes of the corrida, man and bull, are included in Eisenstein's field of vision.

Here—in death, just as there in love—in the twinkling of one radiant moment—solitude and isolation perish.

But in this case the payment for this merging into one is not the destruction of a self-seeking "solitary image" completely dissolving; in this case life is the payment.

The horn pierces man.

Or: shining steel pierces the animal.

There is no other way out.

The price is to perish.

The reckoning is the blood. . . .

Even if the price be blood, man merges with beast.

Even if the price be life, the barriers separating them into distinct categories are torn down.[55]

With his characteristic breadth of inspiration, Eisenstein developed the theme of the corrida almost as if he wished to measure how far the event had extended from the day when, for the first time, in an arena of Crete, this type of spectacle was born: the offering of a victim on behalf of the crowd. In the mystery of Eisenstein's corrida, a victim is offered to the crowd, and the sacrificial lamb is sometimes the matador, sometimes the bull. The succession of changes in the drawings is as rapid as the movements of the matador in the arena. Just a few graphic gestures, and the bull is crucified. But this is only the beginning of the metaphor—a few more gestures, and the former enemies are equal victims. The matador and the bull are (literally) crucified together; both are offered in sacrifice. Eisenstein wanted to present the corrida as the highest point of religious ecstasy and as one of the variations on the theme of the unity of life and death, so closely linked here.

His drawings of the corrida also begin another theme of *Que Viva Mexico!* It seems that in showing crucifixion, Eisenstein was also suggesting the subsequent resurrection—that is, the defeat of death through rebirth. He develops this theme in the epilogue. His drawings of the corrida are the only hint that the crucified matador foreshadows the resurrection theme of the film's finale.

Eisenstein started working on the epilogue before he began filming the fourth and last novella, *Soldadera,* because by then it was early November, the time when Mexico celebrates the Day of the Dead, which was to be the main material for the epilogue. Eisenstein wanted to dedicate the epilogue to José Guadalupe Posada, "the incomparable Posada," as he called this Mexican artist. In his black-and-white prints, accompanied by the texts of popular ballads about the revolution, war, and love, the most common characters were *calaveras*—skeletons. Dressed in various costumes, they promenaded, danced, flirted, argued, fought, and even killed each other. There were the traditional Mexican images, with brutal humor and vitality comprehensible only to Mexicans. Eisenstein sought out the widow of the publisher Arroyo for whom Posada had worked, and bought, for inspiration, over two hundred of the master's prints.

They filmed the Day of the Dead "around and around" Mexico City: dancing *calaveras,* toy skulls, skulls made of sugar, carousing in the cemetery, parades on the streets of the capital. They also staged some shots. Eisenstein

> borrowed skeletons from the medical school in Mexico City, took them to the roof of the Hotel Imperial and dressed them up, some as the characters in the *Maguey* story, others as a banker, a general, a hacendado and an archbishop. . . . His shots of the President, General Calles, and the Archbishop of Mexico were to be intercut with "their" respective skeletons. This Posada-like political satire . . . was to be juxtaposed with the faces of laughing Mexicans . . . children who were the epitome of the future.[56]

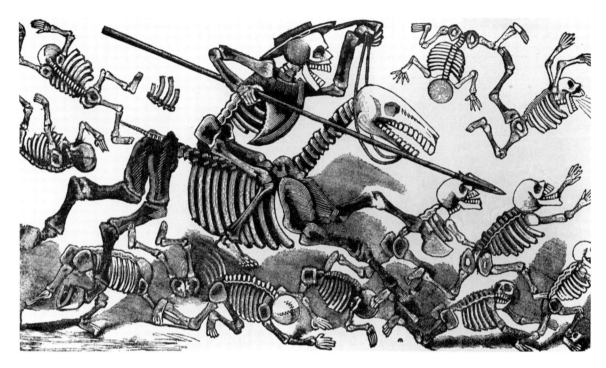

6. *José Guadalupe Posada,* Calavera Don Quijote, *type-metal engraving.*

In the film, in the midst of the carnival all the *calaveras* suddenly strip off the masks of Death. Under some masks are painted skulls; under the others are human faces. The last to remove his mask is an Indian boy—a close-up that fills the screen shows his smiling face. For Eisenstein this image was a metaphor for Mexico's historical immortality, her renewal, a new start. "Everywhere in Mexico life forces its way out from under death; death takes away the obsolete; centuries lie behind, but also the feeling that *nothing* has yet begun, that much is not yet finished, and that from what has just arisen—there is the possibility of everything developing."[57]

Most of the episodes of the epilogue were filmed, but *Soldadera,* the last and the climactic novella of the whole film, remained untouched. Eisenstein needed an extra month for it. He condensed the shooting schedule to the bare minimum:

Desert—10 days; mountains (battle)—10 days; woods and railroad scenes (near Vera Cruz)—5 days; village (at Aztec pyramids)—10 days; army march—5 days. . . . This episode is the story of Soldadera . . . [one of]

26

the women who by . . . hundreds followed the Revolutionary army. . . .[58] Food and the care for the wounded became the responsibility of the soldiers' wives—soldaderas. In a cloud of dust, with their nimble walk so typical of Mexican women, a host of soldaderas flew ahead of the army. Took over villages. Gathered supplies. Baked and threw together simple Mexican dishes, in order to meet the advancing batallions with hot food and a couple of tortillas. And it was the soldadera who darted about in abandoned battlefields, searching among the corpses for her wounded lover, with whom she had frequently even fought side by side, in order to carry him off the field on her shoulders or to bury him, laying out a cross of colored stones on his grave. . . .[59]

Eisenstein read extensively about the Mexican soldaderas and collected a mass of photographs. But the most unforgettable impression he got was from the soldaderas in Orozco's murals at the National Preparatory School in Mexico City, and from the painter's lithographs and drawings. So, *Soldadera* of *Que Viva Mexico!* was to be dedicated to Orozco.

In the script the novella is outlined very generally. Only by gathering together all of Eisenstein's comments on it is it possible to reconstruct the plot of the novella the way he envisioned it:

A soldadera named Pancha is following her soldier—she is his wife, his hearth and home. First she is the wife of a federalist. But he is killed, and she digs his grave with her hands; having covered his body with earth, she lays out a cross of pebbles on it. A soldier in Zapata's army—until recently the enemy—takes her as his wife. Now she follows him as she followed the other. This soldier also dies, at the very moment when her just-born child utters his first cry. Once again life and death, in the Mexican fashion, stand side by side. Pancha, now with her infant, is following another soldier. Together with the army of Villa she enters Mexico City. For Eisenstein the soldadera now becomes the image of the revolutionary Mexico, handed down the line from one leader to the next.

Imagine! 500 women in an endless cactus desert, dragging through clouds of dust household goods, beds, their children, their wounded, their dead, and the white-clad peasant soldiers in straw hats follow them. We show their march into Mexico City—the Spanish Cathedral—the palaces! . . . the meeting of Villa and Zapata . . . with the Cathedral bells ringing the victory of the first revolution. . . .[60]

27

But Eisenstein was not allowed to film *Soldadera*. On Sinclair's orders, all work on the film was halted. It is still not clear whether Sinclair acted entirely on his own or to accommodate demands from Moscow, but the fact remains Eisenstein was prevented from completing his film, his, as he called it, "poem of love, death and immortality for which I have chosen Mexico as the subject matter."[61]

After fourteen months in Mexico, Eisenstein and his crew returned to the U.S. and from there, without delay, on April 19, 1932, departed for Moscow. Thus came the conclusion of

> the strange case of Eisenstein in Mexico . . . of travelling miles and miles by airplane, of hours in oxen carts trundling along resistant roads, of hours of slow moving on donkeys, of caravans of men and cameras marching for months looking for natural sets on snow covered mountain tops and in jungles filled with wild animals, of weeks and weeks of work in terrific heat—making the first cinema story of that country. . . .[62]

Just before his departure from New York, Eisenstein received a telegram from Sinclair, who promised to send the negative and work-print of *Que Viva Mexico!* on the very next ship. Sinclair never kept his promise, but the telegram remained tacked by Eisenstein's desk until the director's death.

Eisenstein's return to his homeland was not a happy one. The campaign to criticize his work and his cinematic method was on the rise. Now it included a number of people who used to be his supporters and friends. Even Alexandrov turned away from him. Tisse, however, always remained by his side.

In July 1934, in a letter to the Latin American writer Victoria Ocampo, Eisenstein wrote:

> My entire Mexican adventure ended in the worst possible disaster. . . . The photography (that is very beautiful) is all that remains—but the whole composition, montage, etc. is completely destroyed by the imbeciles who managed it. . . . I so loved Mexico and it is painful not to be able to express it in this film that's now destroyed. . . . This whole affair so broke my heart that I became disgusted with cinema and have not made another film. Instead I've worked on a big theoretical opus which will be finished in a month. In part, it is the lectures and lessons I gave at the Moscow Cin-

ema University. This fall, for the sake of change, I will probably stage a theatre production, returning to films only in January/February 1936. I hope that by then my heart will be hidden by . . . scars![63]

For several years (he called them "the empty years after *Que Viva Mexico!*") he did not direct films at all; then a chaotic period of ups and downs in his career began: *Bezhin Meadow* (1937) was banned; for *Alexander Nevsky* (1938) he received the Order of Lenin and the Stalin Prize; for *Ivan the Terrible, Part One* (1945), he received another Stalin Prize, but *Part Two* (1946) was condemned, the filmed material for Part Three was destroyed, and the director was compelled to repent publicly. Eisenstein died in February 1948, very soon after his fiftieth birthday.

In all his misfortunes, his illness, and his premature death, it was as if his own prophecy had come true: "Non-Mexicans probably ought not to laugh at death. Whoever dares to laugh is punished by the terrible goddess Coatlicue, whom I have accidentally kicked in the ribs."[64]

Although what happened with *Que Viva Mexico!* was Eisenstein's life's tragedy, the months spent in Mexico were "the time of highest creative excitement for him . . . [which] nourished all [his] subsequent work."[65] Mexico gave him a new angle from which to view the world—the desire not only to look to the future, but also to relive and respect the past, and to see more in the world than just the dialectical process of class struggle.

Mexico made him more contemplative, more aware of the world around him, more attuned to nature. In his youth, he and his peers within the avant-garde believed that only a "machine" and what looks like a "machine" could be beautiful, and that nature was just a formless "building ground."[66] The Mexican landscape, so unlike the flatness of Moscow's environs, attracted him with its diversity and mysteriousness. It had not yet been assimilated by art—Mexican cinematography had hardly come into existence at that time, and to the Mexican monumentalists who were Eisenstein's contemporaries, the landscape did not present a particular interest. In seeking out the most expressive Mexican landscapes for filming, in selecting the most interesting moments in terms of light and the state of nature, in composing shots and individual frames, Eisenstein in many ways resembled Gauguin, who opened Tahiti to European art.

The experience of *Que Viva Mexico!* would later help Eisenstein to recognize and show the mood of Russian landscapes in his films *Alexander Nevsky* and *Bezhin Meadow.* The unfinished Mexican film continued to ignite his creative imagination; its visual motifs and cinematic devices manifested themselves in his subsequent works. Thus it seems the well-known shot from *Ivan the Terrible* with the extreme close-up on Ivan's profile and a long file of Moscovites weaving through a snowy field was influenced by the director's impressions of the endless stream of pilgrims crawling to the shrine of the Lady of Guadalupe in the immense vastness of the Mexican landscape.

In *Ivan the Terrible* there is a further development of the theme of "mask versus face" from the epilogue of *Que Viva Mexico!* At the czar's feast, a young, handsome *oprichnik,* singing a song about the slaughter of the boyars, alternately reveals and hides his face with a mask of a pretty *boyarishna* (a boyar's daughter). The insertion of close-ups of other *oprichniks'* faces, with their frozen expression of brutality and cunning, creates a dramatic face-mask interplay. The scene is full of associations and hints, including the ambiguous seductiveness of the handsome *oprichnik.* In general, the "mask versus face" theme here is more complex, both conceptually and aesthetically, than the bold presentation of it in *Que Viva Mexico!* Yet, the *boyarishna's* mask is a direct offspring from the epilogue of the Mexican film.

Eisenstein also brought into his later works his interest in the ritual aspect of religion, which was revealed to him in Mexico. He belonged to a generation that considered religion to be a prejudice. Mexico did not make him into a believer, but it did arouse in him an interest in the religious rites of the Indians and the liturgy of Christianity. To the great surprise of his friend, the Mexican painter Jean Charlot, the Soviet director "was studying mysticism and the works of Saint Theresa of Avila . . . I was curious of this angle in his thoughts. I think he felt that he was missing something important, but could not fit it into an orthodox Marxist pattern."[67] It seems even that at times Eisenstein almost began to doubt his atheism. "A pity that I do not believe in God"; "only God could help me" are phrases from his Mexican letters. (But from time to time he was unable to refrain from blasphemy, especially in some of his drawings.)

Under the influence of his Mexican experience, he would create in *Ivan the Terrible* scenes of church services in the Kremlin cathedral, and reenact the Christian mystery of the angel who saved three youths from the evil Chaldeans. At some point in the same film, the black-cowled *oprichniks* moving down the cathedral's aisles in effect complete the procession of the Mexican monks that the director filmed, more than ten years earlier, in Merida.

Mexico is mentioned frequently in Eisenstein's writings—his articles, essays, and also in his *Autobiographical Notes*.[68] These were begun in 1940, but the escalating of the Second World War, the evacuation to Central Asia, and the work on *Ivan the Terrible* left no time for the memoirs. Eisenstein turned to them again in 1946, two years before his death, while he was hospitalized with severe cardiac infarction. It happened on November 2, and Eisenstein was quick to point out that this date was the Mexican Day of the Dead.

The memoirs were never completed. In the foreword to his *Autobiographical Notes* Eisenstein stated: "In my creative work through my life, I have been occupied with composing á thèse.[69] I have proved; I have explained; I have taught. Here I simply wish to browse through my own past . . ."[70]

Autobiographical Notes consist of separate fragments about his life, about art, film, people, and places. Their structure rests on associations, rather than themes or chronology. "Some chapters begin with one thing," explained Eisenstein. "Then follows an accidentally emerging reminiscence and, finally, a whole chain of free association. Beginning a chapter, I never know where it will take off to."[71] Thus the story of Eisenstein's visit to the Museum of Ancient Mayan Culture in Chichen Itza one night, when the lights there suddenly went out ("the statues . . . gained in weirdness, absurdity, disproportion, and scale, because they were suddenly snatched out of the darkness by matches struck now here, now there,")[72] unexpectedly shifts to Tolstoy, when the writer describes the effect of lightning flashes illuminating galloping horses. Then Eisenstein again returns to the museum, and from there, through another association, he goes to the statue of Saint Peter in his cathedral in Rome. But there are separate pages and passages in the memoirs wholly devoted to the Day of the Dead, to corridas, and to Mexican artists. These recollections combine factual accuracy with truly poetic feeling.

In my life I have dozed a great deal in highly varied surroundings. Dying from the heat in a flat-bottomed boat, among the sharp-tailed rayfish, in the lagoons of the Campeche bird sanctuaries. Among the vines growing down the treetops, greedily sucking moisture from veinlike waterways, which allowed the tentacles of the Pacific Ocean into the impenetrable palm forests of the Oaxaca massif. In the distance gleamed the eye of a crocodile lying with its upper jaw on the mirrorlike water. I dozed, lulled by the airplane that was taking me from Veracruz to Progreso across the azure waters of the Gulf of Mexico. The even flight of flamingoes glided like pink arrows between us and the emerald surface of the gulf. Drowsiness engulfed me among the sun-scorched bushes near Izamal, bushes growing from the clefts between the countless kilometers of stones, with their peculiar carvings, once the proud cities of the ancient Toltecs, now looking as if they had been overturned and scattered by the hand of some angry giant.[73]

Eisenstein died suddenly, from a massive heart attack. A few hours before his death, one of the last pencil vignettes that he drew on a scrap of paper was a Mexican *calavera*.

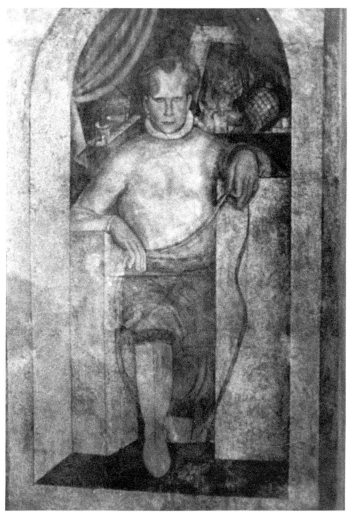

7. *Roberto Montenegro, fresco at the Colegio de Pedro y Pablo in Mexico City, 1931.*
The legend reads "This is Eisenstein." Courtesy of the Colegio de Pedro y Pablo,
Mexico City. (Photo by Carol McCarthy)

"The artichoke looks like a cupola of an Orthodox church. . . .
The resemblance, in fact, is so great that I'm destined to offend the artist Roberto
Montenegro, who painted me in a fresco on a wall of the Teachers' College in Mexico City.
In an image akin to that of Cortes, I'm depicted in front of two baskets with either
pineapples or artichokes. Montenegro is terribly offended. These are not baskets.
They're walls. And those are not pineapples at all, nor, God forbid, artichokes.
They're the cupolas of churches surrounded by the Kremlin wall. A thousand pardons."[74]

II
QUE VIVA MEXICO![75]

The story of this film is unusual.
Four novels framed by prologue and epilogue,
unified in conception and spirit, creating its entity.
Different in content.
Different in location.
Different in landscape, people, customs.
Opposite in rhythm and form, they create a vast and
multicolored Film-Symphony about Mexico.
Six Mexican folk-songs accompany these novels,
which themselves are but songs, legends, tales
from different parts of Mexico brought together
in one unified cinematic work.

8. Eisenstein and Alexandrov at Chichen Itza, Yucatan.
Courtesy of the Lilly Library.

PROLOGUE

Time in the prologue is eternity.

It might be today.

It might as well be twenty years ago.

Might be a thousand.

For the dwellers of Yucatan, land of ruins and huge pyramids, have still conserved, in feature and forms, the character of their ancestors, the great race of the ancient Mayas.

Stones—

Gods—

Men—

Act in the prologue.

In time remote . . .

In the land of Yucatan, among heathen temples, holy cities and majestic pyramids. In the realms of death, where the past still prevails over the present, there the starting-point of our film is laid.

As a symbol of recalling the past, as a farewell rite to the ancient Maya civilization, a weird funeral ceremony is held.

In this ceremony, idols of the heathen temples, masks of the gods, phantoms of the past, take part.

In the corresponding grouping of the stone images, the masks, the bas-reliefs and the living people, the immobile act of the funeral is displayed.

The people bear resemblance to the stone images, for those images represent the faces of their ancestors.

The people seem turned to stone over the grave of the deceased in the same poses, the same expressions of face, as those portrayed on the ancient stone carvings.

A variety of groups that seem turned to stone, and of monuments of antiquity—the component parts of the symbolic funerals—appear in a shifting procession on the screen.

And only the quaint rhythm of the drums of the Yucatan music, and the high-pitched Maya song, accompany this immobile procession.

Thus ends the prologue—overture to the cinematographic symphony, the meaning of which shall be revealed in the contents of the four following stories and of the Finale at the end of these.

9. A shot from the Prologue of Que Viva Mexico!

10. A shot from the Prologue of Que Viva Mexico!

"Faces of stone. And faces of flesh. The man of Yucatan today. The same man who lived thousands of years ago."[76]

11. A shot from the Prologue of Que Viva Mexico!
Courtesy of the Lilly Library.

"As a symbol of recalling the past as a farewell rite to the ancient Maya civilization, a weird funeral ceremony is held."[77]

43

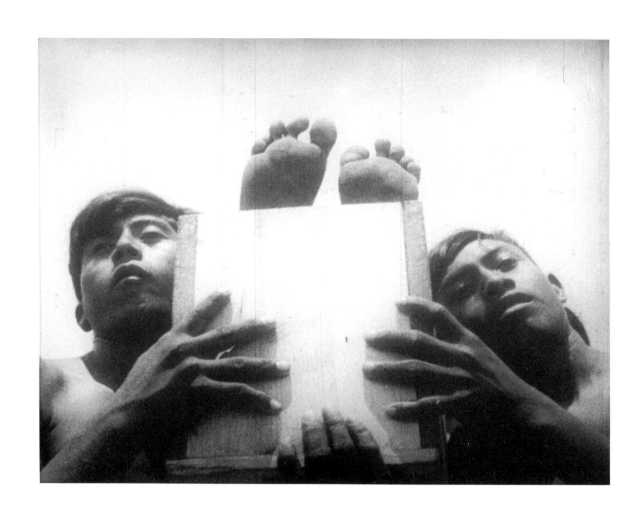

12. A shot from the Prologue of Que Viva Mexico!

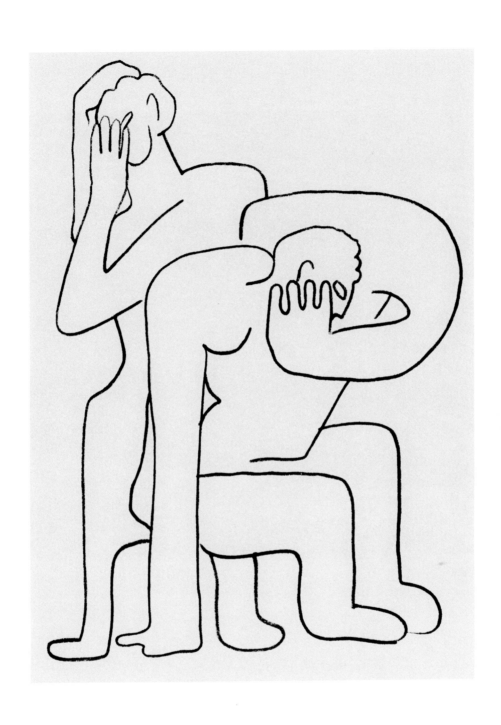

13. Drawing in a "pictograph" style, pencil.

45

14. *A shot from the Prologue (Temple of Quetzalcoatl in Teotihuacan).*
Courtesy of The Museum of Modern Art/Film Stills Archive.

"It is here in tierra caliente *(burning earth) that I come to know the fantastic structure of prelogical, sensuous thinking—not only from the pages of anthropological investigations, but from daily communion with those descendents of the Aztecs and Toltecs, Mayas, or Huichole who have managed to carry unharmed through the ages that meandering thought."*[78]

15. A shot from the Prologue of Que Viva Mexico! *(Yucatan).*
Courtesy of the Lilly Library.

16. A fragment of a shot from the Prologue of Que Viva Mexico! *(Yucatan).*
Courtesy of the Lilly Library.

"You feel almost dizzy when some stone hook protruding diagonally from a building's corner is suddenly recognized as a nose, and then, through the multiplicity of carved stones enveloping the corner you start searching for the eyes."[79]

17. A fragment of a shot from the Prologue of Que Viva Mexico! *(Yucatan).*
Courtesy of the Lilly Library.

18. A shot from the Prologue of Que Viva Mexico! *(Yucatan).*
Courtesy of the Lilly Library.

19. Eisenstein on location for the Prologue of Que Viva Mexico!.

20. *Eisenstein filming an Indian woman's profile against the pyramid of Chichen Itza.*
Courtesy of the Lilly Library.

SANDUNGA

Tropical Tehuantepec.

The Isthmus between Pacific and Atlantic oceans.

Near the borders of Guatemala.

Time is unknown in Tehuantepec.

Time runs slowly under the dreamy weaving of palms and costumes, and customs do not change for years and years.

Persons:

1. Concepcion, an Indian girl
2. Abundio, her novio (future husband)
3. His Mother
4. Tehuanas (Tehuantepec girls)
5. Population of Tehuantepec in festivals, ceremonies, and a popular wedding

Sandunga

The rising sun sends its irresistible call to life.

Its all-pervading rays penetrate into the darkest center of the tropical forest, and, with the sun and the sound of the gentle morning breeze of the ocean, the denizens of the Mexican tropical land awaken.

Flocks of screaming parrots flutter noisily among the palm branches, waking up the monkeys, who close their ears in anger and run down to the river.

On their course these startle the solemn pelicans off the shore sands, and then they plunge, grumbling loudly, into the waves to fish floating bananas and coconuts.

From the deep of the river, crabs, turtles, and sluggish alligators crawl up to the shore to bask their century-old bodies in the sun.

Indian maids are bathing in the river; they lie on the sandy, shallow bottom of the river and sing a song.

Slow as an old-time waltz, sensual as a Danzon, and happy as their own dreams—a Oaxaca song—the *Sandunga*.

Another group of girls in tanned little boats glides slowly by on the bright surface of the river, indulging in the luxury of idleness and the warm kisses of the sunbeams.

A cascade of jet black shining hair drying in the sun denotes a third group of girls seated by the trunks of the nearby palm trees.

Proud and majestic, like a fairy queen in her natural maiden beauty, is among them a girl by the name of Concepcion.

Under the caress of the waves of her hair she lets herself float into dreamland. A wreath of flowers crowns her brow. While listening to the song of her friends she closes her eyes, and in her imagination gold takes the place of flowers.

A necklace of golden coins, adorned with rough pearls strung on threads of golden chains, is glimmering on her breast.

A golden necklace—this is the object of all her dreams; this is the dream of all the Tehuanas—the Tehuantepec girls.

From tender childhood a girl begins to work, saving painstakingly every nickel, every penny, in order that at the age of sixteen or eighteen she may have the golden necklace.

The necklace—that is a fortune, it is an estate. The necklace is the future dowry.

And the bigger, the more expensive it is, the happier future, marital life.

That is why the dreams of Concepcion are so passionate; that is why the visions floating before her mind's eye are so colorful.

Handsome youths alternate with the necklace [in her] dreams.

Youthful beauty blossoms on the screen. . . .

The dreamy song of the girls wafts over the dreamy voluptuous tropics. . . .

Oh, . . . we have let ourselves drift so deeply into dreams, that we have not even noticed how the girls got to work, when they went over to the marketplace, exhibited their wares: oranges, bananas, pineapples, flowers, pots, fish, and other merchandise for sale. The Tehuantepec marketplace is an interesting sight. If you will look in this corner you may think yourself in India.

On turning to the other side, you will find it like Bagdad because of the big earthenware pots surrounding its youthful vendor.

In still another place it looks like the South Seas. However, there are also spots that look like nothing else on earth, for four-eyed fishes are sold only in Tehuantepec.

As soon as a girl sells some trifle, as soon as she receives the few cents in payment, she immediately begins to think of the necklace, begins to count the gold coins she still has to earn.

Thus, coin by coin, the necklace is built, enhanced, but, alas, it is still short one—the bigger, central coin.

So thought Concepcion, she needed only one, just one more coin to win the right to happiness!

Business, however, is slow in the quiet, lazy tropical market.

Concepcion goes on dreaming about this last coin, while the song, the song that stands for happiness with Tehuantepec girls, continues to float in the air.

But at last the bananas are sold, those bananas that were to bring in the money for completion of the necklace. And as the customer pays Concepcion, she says: 'May your necklace bring you luck!'

The happy Concepcion tightly grips the long wished-for coin in her hand . . .

The most beautiful that the tropical forest can yield, flowers, banana-trees, palm-leaves, fruits, adorn the walls of the dance hall.

The most elegantly dressed of the Tehuana girls are seen there. The dance hall is the only place where a youth and a girl may meet, where they can confide to each other the secret of the heart!

In the brilliance of her best dress and the high pitch of her feelings, she casts aside the silk veil of her shawl to draw the eyes of all youths and maidens and keep them spellbound upon the splendor of her beauty and her new golden necklace.

After the dance, when Concepcion withdraws with her beloved to a retired corner, Abundio proposes to her. . . .

Behold Concepcion trembling, pensive, frightened. And here the author speaks!

—Why Concepcion, isn't this what you came for? Is it not what you expected? Is it not what you longed for? In reply to the voice of the author Concepcion smiles, nods her head in assent. But!

The Bridegroom's Mother is a practical woman!

She sends her women to the bride's house to take stock of the dowry and make sure that all is right.

That there are enough petticoats in the trousseau. That the gold coins in the necklace are plentiful.

Experienced old women, nearly centenarians who had taken hand in the marriages of three generations, come to Concepcion's home. They examine all her outfit, feel the velvet, smell the silk, count the gold coins in the necklace and subject them to the tooth-test to make sure of the purity of the gold.

Stirred to the depths of her soul, Concepcion laughs with joy and happiness. The venerable women then pronounce judgment:

All is perfectly right! So, traditional rites begin.

Concepcion's friends bring her presents: A cow dressed up in a masquerade costume; goats with bow ties around their necks; they are carrying on their shoulders many hens, turkeys, little pigs and other gifts and in a quaint procession are advancing toward the bride's home.

In compliance with a tradition centuries old, they bring her pure bee's-wax candles fantastically decorated.

Middle-aged women are busy in the elaborated preparation of typical and delicious dishes for the indispensable, peculiar banquet.

Entire Tehuantepec is stirred up by this event.

All the girls are wearing their fairy regional costumes and wait for the newly-wedded near the church.

Under the sound of the wedding bells the procession carrying palm branches goes to the house of the young couple.

And when left by themselves, Concepcion coyly allows her husband to take off her pride—the golden necklace.

Grandma runs out on the balcony and loudly announces to the expectant Tehuantepecans that Concepcion—the girl—has become Concepcion the woman.

Sky rockets soar up high; fireworks crack, all the young girl friends of Concepcion turn their fairy headgear inside out, like a flock of bih-birds all spreading out their wings, and they dance and sing! . . .

The Sandunga that always sings in the air whenever happiness comes—either in dreams or in reality.

While throughout the tropical forest, under the peaceful fragrance of the palm trees, life pursues its habitual daily course.

The old apes rock their offspring to sleep.

Parrots teach their young to scream.

Pelicans bring fish for their little ones in their pouches.

Time passes, new flowers bloom. Concepcion the woman is now a happy mother.

Thus the story of Concepcion comes to an end, with the portraying of happy, contented parents and a laughing boy.

With the sun setting beyond the ocean.

With the peaceful lyric song of dreaming beautiful girls.

Ends the romance of tropical Tehuantepec.

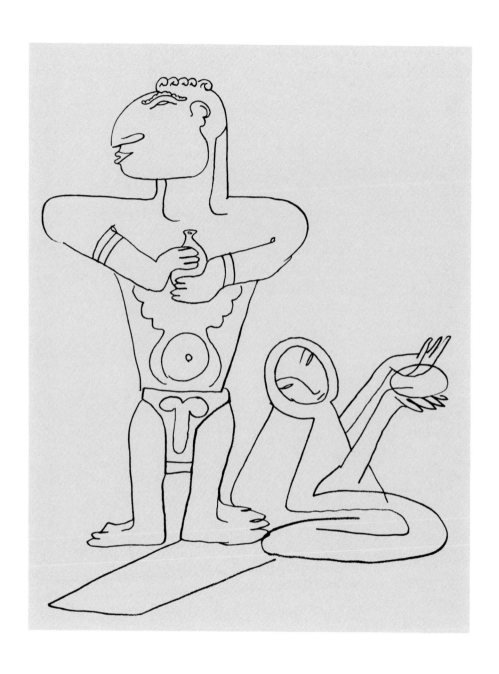

21. Drawing in a "pictograph" style, pencil.

"I did a lot of drawing in Mexico."[80]

58

22. Three figures, pencil.

59

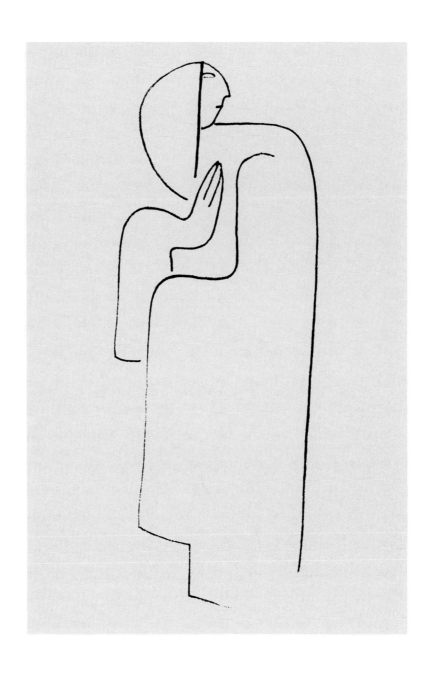

23. A Mayan woman, pencil.

"In Mexico, my drawing went through a stage of inner purification in its striving for a mathematically abstract and pure line . . . the "mathematical" line, so dear to my heart . . . {the line} capable of a whole range of expressiveness."81

60

24. A shot from Sandunga.

25. Conversation, pencil.

26. *A shot from* Sandunga.
Courtesy of the Museum of Modern Art/Film Stills Archive.

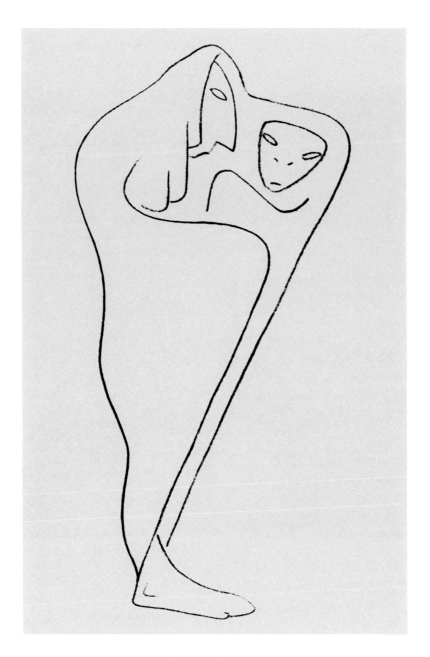

27. Mexican Mother, pencil.

"In my drawing—the influence . . . of all varieties of Mexican primitivism—from the reliefs of Chichen Itza, the primitive toys and the painted household wares, to the inimitable Posada's illustrations of folk songs. . . . For fourteen months I avidly explored {all of these} with my hands and eyes. . . ."[82]

64

28. A shot from Sandunga.

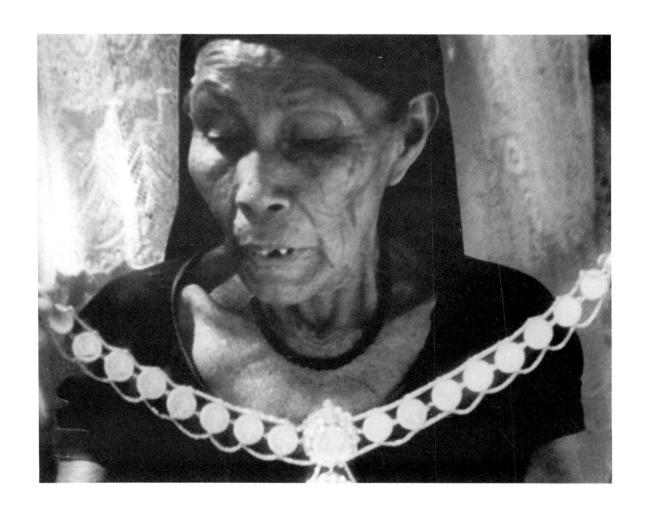

29. A shot from Sandunga.

66

30. Uninterrupted lines, pen and ink.

31. Women from Tehuantepec, pencil.

32. A shot from Sandunga.
Courtesy of the Museum of Modern Art/Film Stills Archive.

"I am now on a thin stretch of land called the Isthmus of Tehuantepec between the Gulf of Mexico and the Pacific . . . shooting for hours at marvellously feminine dark-coloured girls."[83]

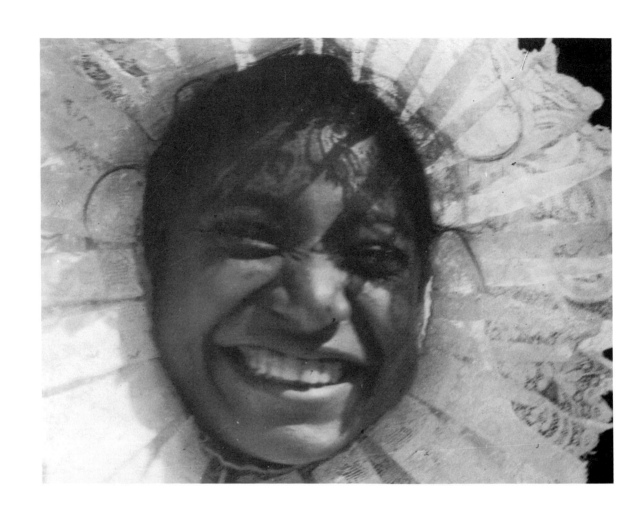

33. A shot from Sandunga.

34. A drawing in a "pictograph" style, pen and ink.

71

35. Eisenstein in Chichen Itza.
Courtesy of the Lilly Library.

36. Eisenstein at the Hacienda Tetlapayac
Courtesy of the Lilly Library

74

MAGUEY

The action of this story develops through the endless fields of maguey in the "Llanos de Apam" and the ancient Hacienda de Tetlapayac, State of Hidalgo. "Llanos de Apam" are the foremost pulque-producing sections of Mexico.

Time of the action, beginning of this century under the social conditions of Porfirio Diaz's dictatorship.

Persons:

1. Sebastian, peon indio
2. Maria, his bride
3. Joaquin, her father
4. Ana, her mother
5. The Hacendado
6. Sara, his daughter
7. Don Julio, her cousin
8. Don Nicolas, the administrator
9. Melesio, his mozo
10. Señor Balderas, a guest
11. Felix
12. Luciano—peons, friends of Sebastian
13. Valerio
14. Charros, mozos, guests, and peons

Aggressiveness, virility, arrogance, and austerity characterize this novel.

As the North Pole differs from the Equator, so unlike to dreamy Tehuantepec are the famous "Llanos de Apam."

So different their people, customs, ways, and mode of living.

At the foot of the high volcanoes, at an altitude of ten thousand feet, on this desert land grows the big cactus plant—the Maguey.

With their mouths the peons suck the juice of this cactus plant to make the Indian drink known as "Pulque."

White, like milk—a gift of the gods, according to legend and belief, this strongest intoxicant drowns sorrows, inflames passions, and makes pistols fly out of their holsters.

Feudal estates, former monasteries of the Spanish conquerors, stand like unapproachable fortresses amidst the vast seas of cactus groves.

Long before dawn, long before the snowy peaks of the volcanoes are lit up by the first rays of the sun, over the high walls of the massive farmhouse come the sad, slow tunes of a song.

El Alabado the peons call this song.

They sing it every morning before they get to work.

It is a hymn in which they pray to the Holy Virgin to help them on the newly dawning day. When the high snowy peaks of the mountains begin to glitter under the rising sun, the gates of the fortress-like farmhouse are opened and, ending their song, the peons tightly wrapped in their serapes and holding their big sombreros in their hands, pour out into the cactus fields to suck in the juice of the maguey with long, especially fitted calabashes.

On the screen you shall see the astonishingly original process of pulque production—which originated hundreds of years ago and has not changed up to the epoch of this story.

Later, when the fog has cleared away, when the sun has warmed the earth, the servants of the landlord's household get up and begin preparations for the evening, for on this day the annual feast of the Hacienda is to be celebrated.

The charros put on their best costumes in honor of the guests and they exhibit boastfully their remarkable horses.

Meantime, in the maguey field, where the peon Sebastian is working, a meeting takes place. Maria's parents bring their daughter to hand her over to her *fiancé*.

According to tradition, Sebastian will have to take his bride to the owner of the Hacienda as homage.

But the charros who are guarding the landlord's house won't let Sebastian in, so he has to remain in the front yard.

On the terrace the landlord, in the company of a group of his nearest friends, are having drinks—and their spirits are rising.

The hacendado receives Maria; he is a good-natured old man; he fumbles in his vest pocket for a few pesos as a gift to the bride.

But at this moment an old-fashioned carriage drawn by six mules comes speeding along.

The old man's daughter, Sara, has arrived.

She has brought her cousin with her and has broken in upon the group on the veranda in a storm of laughter and gaiety.

She flies into her father's arms. And all their friends drink a toast to her health.

Maria is forgotten.

Sebastian gets restless, while waiting in the front yard.

His sweetheart is slow in coming back to him and the explosive laughter on the veranda sounds suspicious.

The forgotten, frightened, inexperienced Maria is awaiting her luck.

Bad luck appears in the shape of a coarse, drunken guest with a big moustache.

Availing himself of the fact that the company is too absorbed with drinking and merry-making, he seizes Maria from behind a door and drags her into a remote room.

One of the servants, a close friend of Sebastian, witnesses this scene and runs with all his might to the yard with his startling news.

The Indian blood of Sebastian dictates his further course of action.

He rushes up the veranda knocking the guards off their feet, he breaks in like a storm among the merry guests. . . .

He demands Maria, his bride.

A fight starts at once, but is brought just as quickly to an end, for slim are the chances of Sebastian alone against all the assemblage.

Sebastian is sent rolling down the stairs for his insolence and effrontery.

A door opens and the intoxicated villain appears before the excited group. Distraught, weeping, Maria slips by stealthily behind his back.

The tenseness of the situation is aggravated. But the hacendado is a good-natured old man. He does not want to mortify his guests, he does not want to spoil the feast.

To distract the people he issues orders to start the music, the fireworks, and the games.

Maria is put under lock till next morning, pending the hearing of the case.

In the rattle of the music, the excitement of the games and intoxication of hilarity, the sad incident is forgotten.

The brighter the fireworks blaze, the more violent wrath rages within Sebastian's heart.

Vengeance germinates in his mind.

Vengeance begets conspiracy.

Three of his comrades pledge themselves to help him get revenge.

In an auspicious moment they direct the blazing sky-rockets into hay-stacks.

The flames spread like wild fire.

While the assemblage is panic-stricken, Sebastian and his associates provide themselves with arms and cartridges out of the landlord's supplies and make an attempt to release Maria from confinement.

But the guards fire back and the conspirators are forced to flee.

Under cover of night the fugitives evade persecution.

Morning overtakes them in a forest on the slope of a mountain.

Wending their way towards the mountain pass across the ridges, they plod laboriously through the thickest of the fairy-woods. The charros, however, on their fine horses, accompanied by the indomitable Sara and her cousin, make the pass first and intercept the fugitives.

Cross-firing breaks out in the tangle of the nopal-wood.

Sara, fascinated by the shooting, incessantly makes attempts to rush forward, and her cousin has to keep her back at a distance from the whizzing bullets by sheer force.

Sara kills one of the peons and pays with her life for her daring.

A bullet finds its way to her heart through the watch she is so fond of. The mechanism of the broken watch trembles under the shots and slowly stops its movement.

Sara's cousin puts her body across his saddle and carries her away from the field of battle.

The shooting breaks out anew with increased violence.

The fugitives are retreating into the maguey fields.

In the stronghold of a huge cactus, three of them seek refuge.

The hissing bullets pierce the succulent leaves of the maguey plant and the juice, like tears, trickles down its trunk.

The cartridges are exhausted.

The peons make an attempt to flee.

The agile charros fling their lassos around the fugitives and hold them captives.

All torn, tottering Sebastian and two of his surviving friends are brought in upon the scene of Sara's funeral.

Eye for an eye . . . they pay with their lives for their daring.

Among the magueys, where Sebastian had worked and loved, he finds his tragic end. . . .

Beyond the great snow-white summits of the volcanoes the sun is sinking. The day is dying.

The large gates of the estate are closing.

Maria is set at liberty and goes looking for the body of Sebastian amidst the maguey plants.

Her appearance startles the buzzards and they fly away.

While over the high walls of the estate float the sounds of wailing.

A mournful, drawn-out wailing—the Indian farewell to the setting sun.

Maria finds the remains of her beloved, of him who was to become her husband, who had raised his arm in her defence . . . she sobs convulsively over his dead body.

Beyond the tall walls of the hacienda the peons are singing their vesper song—just as plaintive, as mournful, as their morning Alabado.

37. A shot from Maguey.
Courtesy of the Academy of Motion Picture Arts and Sciences.

38. A shot from Maguey.
Courtesy of the Academy of Motion Picture Arts and Sciences.

"The real Mexico ten years after I conjured up its image in my first theatrical work."[84]

81

39. Maguey, work photograph.
Courtesy of the Museum of Modern Art/Film Stills Archive.

"The Hacienda Tetlapayac. Here, on the estate of Señor Julio Saldivar and his grandfather, we are shooting scenes of the peon uprising for our Mexican film."[85]

82

40. Serape, colored pencil.

"Do you know what a 'serape' is? A serape is the striped blanket that . . . every Mexican wears. So striped and violently contrasting are the cultures in Mexico running next to each other and at the same time being centuries away. . . ."[86]

41. Three peones, colored pencil.

84

42. Sombrero, colored pencil.

"The amazingly clear linear order of the Mexican landscape, the white square clothing of the peon, the rounded outlines of his straw hat. . . ."[87]

43. A fragment of a shot from Maguey.
Courtesy of the Museum of Modern Art/Film Stills Archive.

"The peon Martin Fernandez in the role of the peon Sebastian. 'Torito'—the traditional firecracker bull at Mexican national festivals. People put them on their heads, to parody bullfight. It shoots rockets (especially powerful ones spew from the horns)."[88]

86

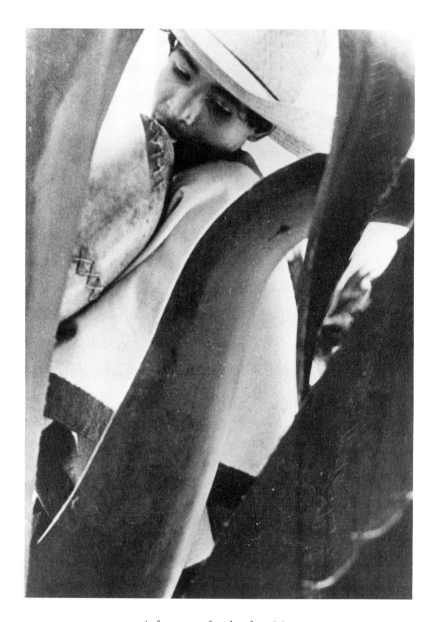

44. *A fragment of a shot from* Maguey.
Courtesy of the Academy of Motion Picture Arts and Sciences.

"The sand boiling in the blazing sun, the sand that collects the vital juices of the desert into the unexpected miracle of the fruits of the palmate cactus: A knife cuts across these pulpy clusters, which serve as pedestal for the dazzling rose flowers of the cactus, and teeth greedily bite into the violet piece of sweet ice—so cold is this fruit, growing in the very heart of a sandy hell . . . the desert scorched by the sun."[89]

45. A shot from Maguey.
Courtesy of the Academy of Motion Picture Arts and Sciences.

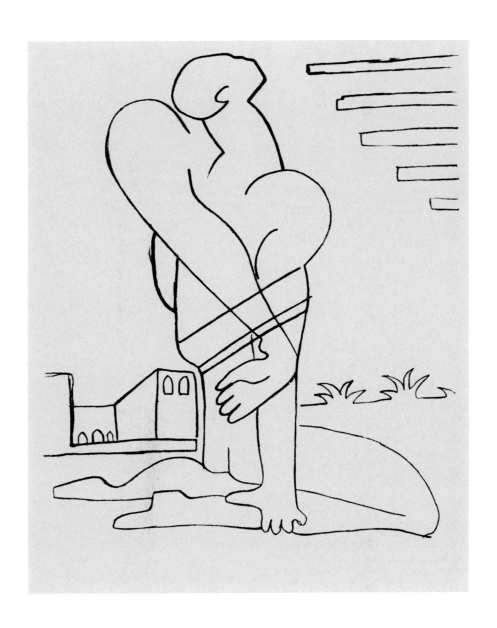

46. Execution, pencil.

47. A shot from Maguey.

48. A shot from Maguey.

49. *Eisenstein filming* Maguey.
Courtesy of the Lilly Library.

50. *Eisenstein and Tisse filming a scene for* Fiesta, *Merida.
Courtesy of the Museum of Modern Art/Film Stills Archive.*

THE FIESTA

Time of the action—same as *Maguey*—that is—prior to the Revolution of 1910.

Action includes scenery of all the most beautiful spots of Spanish colonial style and influence in art, buildings and people in Mexico.

(Mexico City, Xochimilco, Merida, Taxco, Puebla, Cholula, etc.)

The atmosphere of this part is of pure Spanish character.

Persons:

1. Baronita, picador and first lover
2. The Matador (played by champion matador David Liceaga)
3. Señora Calderón, one of the queens at the bullfight
4. Señor Calderón, her husband
5. Hundreds of ritual dancers, danzantes in front of the Basilica de Guadalupe
6. Crowds of pilgrims and penitents

Crowds enjoying the bullfight and the floating gardens of the Mexican Venice—Xochimilco

The Fiesta

Weirdness, romance, and glamour constitute the make-up of the third novel.

The Spanish colonial *barroco* works the stone into fanciful lacework on the

95

wire ribbon of columns and church altars. Thus the complex designs, the elaborate composition of this episode.

All the beauty that the Spaniards have brought with them into Mexican life appears in this part of the picture.

Spanish architecture, costumes, bullfights, romantic love, southern jealousy, treachery, facility at drawing the gun, manifest themselves in this story.

In old prerevolutionary Mexico the annual holiday in worship of the Holy Virgin of Guadalupe is taking place.

Hence the abundance of merry-go-rounds, shows, flowers, the multitudes of people. Pilgrims from all parts of the country are coming to the feast.

Dancers of ritual dances are getting their fantastic costumes and masks ready.

The bishops and archbishops are donning their gorgeous robes.

The girls who are destined to appear as queens of the bullfights are putting on their expensive combs and mantillas in a tremor of vanity.

And finally the heroes of this tale, the famous matadors, are getting dressed for the performance on the veranda of a Spanish patio, amid the tinkling of guitars and the sound of militant songs of the ring.

The best of the matadors is enacted by David Liceaga, the most renowned matador of Mexico and "champion" of the "golden ear."

In front of a pier-glass, swelling with the self-consciousness of their importance and grandeur, the matadors are putting on their gold and silk embroidered costumes.

More than the others, wriggles in front of the mirror (the most concerned about his personal appearance), the care-free picador, the lazy Don Juan Baronita.

He is mindful of every detail, for an encounter more hazardous than the bullfight awaits him.

He has a date with another man's wife! Having dressed, the matadors drive to the chapel of the Holy Virgin, the patron of their dangerous art.

Having knelt before her altar, whispered to her his prayer, and begged her benediction, the best of the great matadors drives over to the quiet home of his mother to bid her—

Goodbye!

Maybe for the last time—

And on the plaza a multitude of some sixty thousand people, amid hand-clapping, shouts its impatience. The orchestra in gayful tunes begins to play the opening official march and the matadors make their appearance in the arena.

During the parade the picador Baronita appears in full splendor, mounted on his white horse, and throws a stealthy glance in the direction where the queens are seated.

The belles of the city in expensive lace under the refreshing breeze of fans, and open coquetry, are filling the "Royal" box seats.

Baronita manages to locate the queen of his inflamed heart and give her his "killing" glance.

And as in the traditional *Carmen* the eyes of the matadors meet the dark eyes of the beautiful queens and as a tradition dictates, this glance kindles the flame of valour in the matadors' eyes.

The sixty thousand attendants release an *Ah!* of wonder the moment the bull runs out into the ring. The very famous David Liceaga displays all the beauty and elegance of the art of the matador.

Full of grace and valour he dances his "dance" on the margin of death and triumph.

He does not stir from his place even when the bull's horns come within a hair's breadth of his body; he does not tremble, but smiles serene, and to top it all he pets the sharp horns of the animal and this provokes an endless savage outburst of delight from the crowd.

But the bull, enraged by the teasing of Liceaga knocks down the horse of the infatuated Baronita.

And he is forced disgracefully to jump the enclosure under the roars of derisive laughter from the crowd.

Notwithstanding all this, his love remains true to him—she gives him the high sign of the feasibility of their rendezvous.

In the meantime, in the town square, fairs and market-places, a crowd of many thousands are contemplating the ritual ceremonial dances of Indians dressed up in gilded brocade, ostrich feathers, and huge masks.

Under the peals of the ancient Spanish church bells, under the sound of music and the rolling of beating drums, the thunder of exploding sky rockets, the feast flourishes. Under the roar of the exalted crowd, at the other place, the killed bull is taken away from the grounds.

A maelstrom of hats and unabating ovations accompany the triumphant exit of the valiant matador.

Baronita has now met his "queen." Wrapped up in one cloak, the pair of lovers make their way through the narrow Spanish alleys to the landing of the boats adorned with flowers.

Their boat sails by the floating gardens along the dreamland canals of Xochimilco, the so-called Venice of Mexico.

In the shade of an awning under the sound of guitars and marimbas the pair of lovers will forget their troubles.

But trouble does not forget them.

The wife catches sight of her husband; the pair hide behind the curtain and a swift change of their course saves them from a tragic fate.

The husband is furious, he is raving, because he can find no trace of his wife. A mad pursuit among the moving maze of flower-covered floating temples of love. . . .

The boat of the amorous pair passes under his very nose and disappears among hundreds of other festively adorned boats.

In a retired nook of a remote canal the "Ship of Love" lands. Baronita conducts his forbidden love to the summit of a mountain, to a big stone crucifix, where they watch the sunset and exchange kisses.

In their moment of utmost bliss they are surprised by the husband. He draws his Spanish fancy-made pistol. He is ready to discharge it. And by pure miracle Baronita escapes the avenging hand. . . .

The final song of the great feast ends the day.

Happy, romantic is the finale of the story about this ancient and beautiful Spanish holiday.

51. The Conquest, pencil.

52. *A shot from* The Fiesta.

53. A shot from The Fiesta.

54. A shot from The Fiesta.

55. *A shot from* The Fiesta.
Courtesy of the Museum of Modern Art/Film Stills Archive.

"*The Catholic asceticism . . . imposing the iron heel of fire and blood upon the sensual
splendor of . . . Mexico.*"[90]

56. *Two figures, pencil.*

105

57. A nun, pencil.

LA FUITE EN EGYPTE.

58. The flight to Egypt, pencil.

59. Madonna and the Child, pencil.

60. *Madonna, collage.*

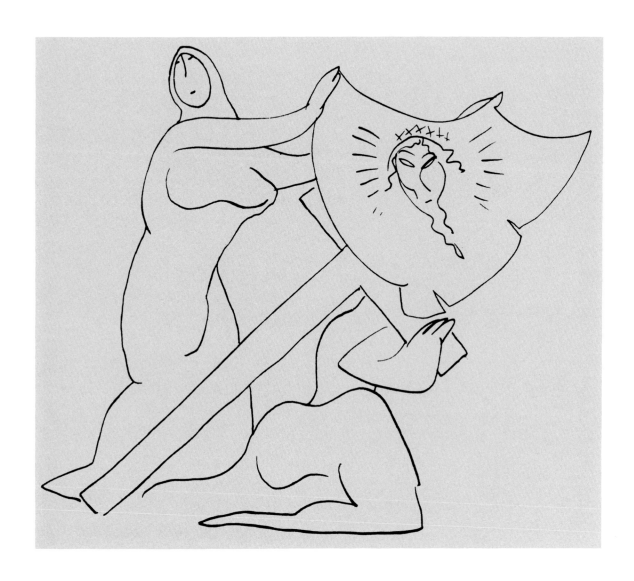

61. St. Veronica, pen and ink.

62. *A shot from* The Fiesta.

63. *A shot from* The Fiesta.
Courtesy of the Museum of Modern Art/Film Stills Archive.

"Streams of pilgrims, on their knees crawling up the pyramids
crowned with Catholic cathedrals. . . .
On the pilgrims' path, at separate turns along the road, stand stone reminders of the
Twelve Stations of Christ's way to Golgotha.
And by each of these markers, a crowd of pilgrims rehearse silently
the corresponding episode from the drama of Christ's Passion so well known to all."[91]

64. The Crucifixion, pencil.

65. *Eisenstein and Liceaga on location, Merida.*
Courtesy of the Lilly Library.

66. *Corrida, collage.*

"The bullfight is in full swing. The barbaric splendor of this sport of blood, gilt and sand attracts me madly."[92]

67. A shot from The Fiesta.
Courtesy of the Lilly Library.

116

68. Admiration for the Matador, pen and ink.

69. A shot from The Fiesta.
Courtesy of the Museum of Modern Art/Film Stills Archive.

70. The Matador, pen and ink.

71. A shot from The Fiesta.

72. Bull and Matador, pen and ink.

73. *A shot from* The Fiesta.

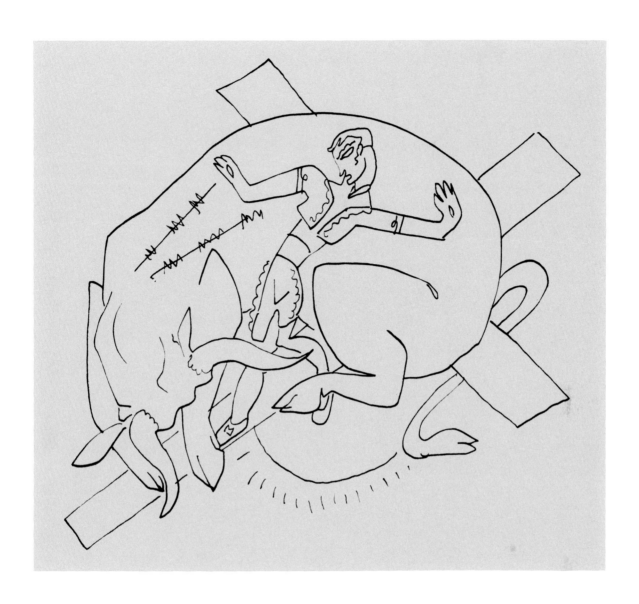

74. *Crucifixion of the Matador* (1), *pen and ink.*

*"The matador, who in the simultaneous attempt of the bull and man to rush at each
other, pierces with his sword like a flash of lightning into the blackness splashed with
foam, the blackness of the fiery element of the horned monster. . . . The horn or sword
penetrate each other; they penetrated each other in a similar great moment of the mutual
merging of life and death, bull and man, instinct and craft:
animal nature and the art of man."*[93]

75. Crucifixion of the Matador (2), pen and ink.

76. Crucifixion of the Matador (3), pen and ink.

77. *Eisenstein in Merida.*

SOLDADERA

The background of this story is the tumultuous canvas of uninterrupted movements of armies, battles, and military trains which followed the revolution of 1910 until peace and the new order of modern Mexico were established.

Deserts, woods, mountains, and the Pacific Coast at Acapulco, and Cuautla, Morelos, are the landscapes of this story.

Persons:

1. Pancha, the woman who follows the soldier—the Soldadera
2. Juan, Pancha's soldier
3. The sentinel, Pancha's second soldier
4. Pancha's child
5. The Army in march and fight
6. Hundreds of soldaderas, wives of the soldiers, following the armies

Soldadera

Yells, shouts, general havoc seem to reign in the small Mexican village.

At first one gets bewildered, one cannot understand what is going on—women are catching hens, pigs, turkeys; women are hastily seizing tortillas and chile in the houses.

128

Women wrangling, fighting, shouting at each other. . . .

What is up?

These are soldiers' wives, soldaderas, forerunners of the army, who have invaded the village.

Those are the soldaderas getting provisions to feed their weary husbands.

One of them is Pancha; a machine-gun ribbon hangs across her shoulder, a big sack containing household utensils weighs heavily on her back. . . .

Having caught a chicken and voiced her snappish retort to the protests of its owner, she finds a convenient place for the day's quarters.

The soldaderas are breaking camp by the bridge on the bank of the river, they are getting their [grinding-stones]—*metates*—out of their sacks, are husking corn, kindling fires, and the clapping of their palms, patting tortillas into shape, seems to announce peace.

A little girl is crying and to console her, the mother, for lack of candy, gives her a cartridge.

The child sucks at the dum-dum bullet and rejoices over the glistening toy.

The weary army enters the village, and the soldiers in ravenous anticipation inhale the smoke of the bonfires.

Clarions sound the call to rest.

Artillery soldiers release the donkeys and mules from the dust-covered machine-gun carriages; the women are looking for their men.

Pancha finds her soldier, Juan.

She treats him to a roast chicken and hot tortillas.

Supper over, Juan rests his head in Pancha's lap and hums the tune the guitars are playing.

Adelita is the name of the song and this song is the leitmotif of the Soldadera.

When overcome by exhaustion he falls asleep, and his stentorian snoring joins in the general snoring chorus of sleeping soldiers.

Pancha washes his shirt—and cleans his gun.

At dawn, while the echo of the desert still reverberates with the soldiers' snoring, Pancha places five or six cartridges in Juan's gun and puts the gun by his side.

She packs her household belongings in her big sack and lifting it to her back she joins the crowd of women setting out on their endless pilgrimage.

129

Faint under their heavy loads, trying to calm the crying children, munching the tortillas left over from breakfast, the crowd of women runs along the dusty, deserted road.

Suddenly the loud voice of the author calls to Pancha:

—Say, Soldadera. . . .

Pancha stops, turns her head toward the camera, first she just stares; then, pointing her finger to her breast, she inquires silently: "Did he call her?" The Voice, again:

"Where art thou going, woman?"

She turns pensive, smiles enigmatically, shrugs her shoulders, as if ignorant of what to answer, parts her hands in the broad gesture women are apt to make when saying:

—"Who knows?" (*Quien sabe* . . . ?)

She is borne onwards by the strong current of women and gets lost in the big moving mass of humanity and in the dust that veils everything from the human eye.

Machine-guns are roaring.

The clatter of cavalry is heard.

A battle is raging.

Juan is fighting like all the rest of the soldiers.

He discharges his gun.

Shouts . . . *"ora . . . arriba . . . Adelante."* . . .

Rushes into attack amidst bursting shells.

Under the cars of a freight train the soldaderas are praying for their fighting men.

They have suspended their Santos—the holy images of their dearest devotion—from the car wheel and placed their little votive lamps on the springs of the car axle.

The machine-guns are silent.

The shooting abates.

The soldiers' shouts are no longer heard.

The soldaderas go to the head of the train, to the engine, and hence they look in the direction of the ending battle.

The soldaderas rush up to meet [the soldiers], scrutinize their faces.

Question . . . ! "Have you seen mine?"

The excited Pancha is looking for Juan.

Here they bring him wounded.

Pancha runs up to him.

Uncovers his face . . .

No, that is not he . . .

The soldaderas bandage up wounds, treat them to the best of their knowledge. Apply tortillas to the wounds and fasten them with willow fibres.

Juan is safe and sound but worn out, and he must get into the car of his troop, for the officers and engines are blowing the whistles for departure.

Having seen him board the train, Pancha gets on the engine platform.

The angry voice of the sentinel calls to her.

"What have you there under your shawl?"

And lifting her rebozo, Pancha answers quietly:

"Who knows, señor, it may be a girl or it may be a boy. . . ."

The troops start off noisily. In the packed cars the soldiers are singing *Adelita!* And on the roofs, the soldaderas with their kitchen [utensils] and children are squatted like crows.

They have kindled bonfires on the iron roofs and the patting of palms making tortillas seems to compete with the rattling of the car wheels.

The military train vanishes into the dark of night.

At daybreak the soot-covered stoker leaps from car to car of the train in motion—jumps among the women and children.

On one of the cars he drops flat on his belly and shouts through the open door. . . .

In answer to his call Juan, aided by his comrades, climbs up to the roof.

The rattling of the train drowns the words of the message the stoker has brought to Juan.

They run fast to the engine, frightening the sprawled women and on reaching their destination, they climb to the front platform.

Under the clothes hung out near the lanterns to dry, under soldiers' underwear waved by the wind, near the blazing bonfire, Pancha is sitting with her newborn baby.

And the same cross guard seated close by, near a machine-gun, asks Pancha:

"Is it a girl or a boy?"

Among the mountains in the clouds, puffing with effort on the steep stretches of the road, the military train is advancing.

Another battle . . . !

Again the racket of machine-guns. . . .

Again the soldaderas are awaiting the returning wounded soldiers. . . .

This time Juan does not come back.

And when the fight is over amidst its smoking ruins Pancha finds the body of her husband. . . .

She gathers a pile of rocks, makes him a primitive tombstone, weaves him a cross of reeds. . . .

She takes his gun, his cartridge belt, his baby, and follows the slowly advancing, tired army.

Her legs can hardly support her body, heavy under the burden of grief and weariness.

And then the same cross soldier walks up to her and takes the baby from her.

Pancha leans on the strong arm of her new husband in order not to fall and not to lag behind the army.

Adelita is the tune the tired bands are playing, falsely and out of rhythm.

The army has prepared for an attack, but the people from the city come up and explain.

The civil war is over.

Revolution has triumphed.

There is no need now of Mexicans fighting Mexicans.

The brass band discovers a new source of strength that enables it to play *Adelita* stoutly, solemnly and triumphantly.

Like peals of thunder roll the triumphant shouts above the heads of the soldiers.

The armies are fraternizing.

One might decipher on the banner—the last word of its device.

Towards Revolution.

Towards a New Life . . . says the voice of the author.

Towards a New Life! . . .

The novella *Soldadera* was never filmed, so the visual material for it does not exist. Below is a letter Eisenstein wrote to Salka Viertel, an actress and a screenwriter. Eisenstein befriended her and her husband, the film director Berthold Viertel, during his stay in Hollywood. Later, while Eisenstein was shooting his film in Mexico, he asked Salka to be his representative when the rushes were shown to the sponsors in Los Angeles.

In her book, *The Kindness of Strangers,* Salka Viertel writes: "As [Eisenstein] had no facilities in Mexico for developing the film, the negative was sent to the Eastman Laboratory in Los Angeles. The Mexican Consul had to see the rushes to be sure that nothing detrimental to Mexico had been filmed. My job was to explain . . . why Eisenstein had photographed this or that from different angles. . . . This film material was stunning . . . breathtakingly beautiful. But the sponsors were indignant that a scene or a place . . . was shot so many times. . . . It was useless to explain that, even unedited, the film revealed Eisenstein's intentions and also the passion and concentration with which he worked. Then suddenly I was no longer told when the rushes were to be shown, and a letter from Eisenstein informed me of what had happened:[94]

27 JANUARY 1932[95]

DEAR ZALKA!

It seems to be your fate that I should be heaping my despair upon you! In my Paramount days and after—but this time is the most desperate of all! I don't know how much Sinclair keeps you *au courant* about our activities and difficulties. If he does I may be as doomed in your eyes as I am in his. However, this is the situation:

You know that instead of the four months schedule and $25,000, which would have merely resulted in a pitiful travelogue we have worked thirteen months and have spent $53,000, but we have a great film and have expanded the original idea. This expansion was achieved under incredible difficulties inflicted upon us by the behavior and bad management of Upton Sinclair's brother-in-law, Hunter Kimbrough. I am blamed for all sin committed and I accept it, under the condition that from now on I myself should be responsible, but not Mr. Kimbrough. Or we three: I, Alexandrov and Tisse, should manage the whole thing until its completion. But I am facing a situation which, so far, had been completely unknown to me: blood relationship and family ties. Mr. Kimbrough was recalled, but then sent back with "increased powers" *as my supervisor,* which means that now he has the right to interfere in everything I do and make all the cuts! He presented me to Sinclair as a liar, blackmailer and God-knows-what else. My direct correspondence with Sinclair stopped, our only contact was through Kimbrough who, an ambitious man, poisons our existence and creates an atmosphere in which it is impossible to work. I wrote this to Sinclair, whereupon he abruptly halted our work of thirteen months. The last part of my film, containing all the elements of a fifth act, is ruthlessly ripped out, and *you* know what this means. It's as if Ophelia were ripped out from *Hamlet,* or King Philip from *Don Carlos.*

We saved this episode, the best material, story and effects, which have not been exploited before, as a climax and the last to be filmed. It tells the story of the *Soldadera,* the women who, in hundreds, followed the Revolutionary army, taking care of their men, bearing them children, fighting at their side, burying them and taking care of the survivors. The incomparable drama and pathos of this sequence shows the birth of the new country. Exploited and suppressed by the Spaniards, it emerges as a free Mexico. Without this sequence the film loses its meaning, unity and its final dramatic impact: it becomes a display of unintegrated episodes. Each of these episodes now points toward this end and this resolution.

Now to our practical achievements: We have 500 soldiers, which the Mexican Army has given us for 30 days, 10,000 guns and 50 cannons, *all for nothing.* We have discovered an incredible location and have brilliantly solved the whole event in our scenario. We need only $7,000 or $8,000 to finish it, which we could do in a month, and then we would have a truly marvelous film—and when I say it I *mean* it!—a film with such mass scenes as no studio could attempt to produce now! Imagine! 500 women in an endless cactus desert, dragging through clouds of dust, household goods, beds, their children, their wounded, their dead, and the white-clad peasant soldiers in straw hats following them. We show their march into Mexico City—the Spanish Cathedral—the palaces! For the meeting of Villa and Zapata we will have thousands of sports organizations—again without pay—with the ca-thedral bells ringing the victory of the first revolution. And all that has to be sacrificed because of $8,000, and quarrels—by the way, I am absolutely right and have documents to prove it—Sinclair stopped the production and intends to throw before the people a truncated stump with the heart ripped out!

I have exhausted my powers of persuasion. I shall do everything he wants. . . . I accept Kimbrough, everything, anything . . . if only they let me finish this film. I have worked under most incredible harassment, no, not worked—fought. When I see you in Hollywood I will tell you what we had to go through and what probably is still ahead of us.

I myself am incapable of persuading these people. Zalka, you have already helped in this cause. We, all three of us, are convinced that this is our best film and that it must not be destroyed. I beg you, Zalka, go to Sinclair. As you were authorized to see all the rushes, he will certainly use the occasion to pour out to you everything which caused the present situation; or better, you could ask him and I am sure influence him. . . . A film is not a sausage which tastes the same if you eat three-quarters of it or the whole *Wurst*. You will hear horrible things about me (first, they are not true, and second, I know you don't care and I beg you to think only about the film). The situation is different now. I have an ironclad plan. I know the locations precisely; General Calles has promised us all the facilities: those are concrete things! And we are now familiar with conditions here and know exactly how to handle the production. Use your Medea flame and convince him (but especially *her*) to let us finish our film.

We were due to leave but Kimbrough postponed our departure for ten days, to clean up odds and ends of what we have shot. Our only hope is that meanwhile a miracle will happen and that the Soldadera episode will be filmed. Help us, Zalka! No, not us, help our work, save it from mutilation! If they have no money, ask for their consent to let us get it elsewhere. It seems incredible that this amount could not be raised as business. Even here the money could be found, not from philanthropists, but from businessmen, but the Sinclairs are so frightened of businessmen that they prefer to destroy all that they now have.

Wire immediately that you have received this letter and that you take our cause to your heart, regardless of what they tell you about me. One does not write such letters often.

Your,
SERGEI

Salka could not persuade the Sinclairs to continue funding the film. And even when, at her urging, David O. Selznick offered to buy out all the material that had been shot, cover all of the Sinclairs' expenses, and finance the rest of the shooting and production of *Que Viva Mexico!* they refused. "Mrs. Sinclair was adamant. She was determined to call an end to the Mexican venture, and that was that," wrote Salka Viertel.[96]

Upon his leaving the United States, Eisenstein wrote to her: "I am very sad because I am not going to see you anymore. . . . You have helped me in the most difficult years of my life and this shall never be forgotten."[97]

78. Eisenstein and the costumed skeleton on location for the Epilogue of
Que Viva Mexico!
Courtesy of the Museum of Modern Art/Film Stills Archive.

EPILOGUE

Time and location—modern Mexico.

Mexico of today on the ways of peace, prosperity and civilization.

Factories, railroads, harbors with enormous boats; Chapultepec, castle, parks, museums, schools, sports-grounds.

The people of today.

Leaders of the country.

Generals.

Engineers.

Aviators.

Builders of new Mexico.

and

Children—the future people of future Mexico.

The work of factories.

The hissing of aeroplane propellers.

The whistles of work-plants.

Modern . . . Civilized . . . Industrial Mexico appears on the screen.

Highways, dams, railways . . .

The bustle of a big city.

New machinery.

New houses.

New people.

Aviators.

Chauffeurs.

Engineers.

Officers.

Technicians.

Students.

Agriculture experts.

And the Nation's leaders, the President, generals, secretaries of State Departments. Life, activity, work of new, energetic people . . . but if you look closer, you will behold in the land and in the cities the same faces—

Faces that bear close resemblance to those who held a funeral of antiquity in Yucatan, those who danced in Tehuantepec; those who sang the Alabado behind the tall walls, those who danced in queer costumes around the temples, those who fought and died in the battles of revolution.

The same faces—

but different people.

A different country,

A new, civilized nation.

But, what is that?

After the bustle of factory machines.

After the parading of modern troops.

After the President's speeches and the generals' commands—

Death comes along dancing!

Not just one, but many deaths; many skulls, skeletons . . .

What is that?

That is the Carnival pageant.

The most original, traditional pageant, "Calavera," death day.

This is a remarkable Mexican day, when Mexicans recall the past and show their contempt of death.

The film began with the realm of death.

With victory of life over death, over the influences of the past, the film ends.

Life brims from under the cardboard skeletons, life gushes forth, and death retreats, fades away.

A happy little Indian carefully removes his death-mask and smiles a contagious smile—he impersonates the new growing Mexico.

79. A shot from the Epilogue.

80. Ecstasy, colored pencil.

81. *Dancing figures, pencil.*

82. A shot from the Epilogue.
Courtesy of the Museum of Modern Art/Film Stills Archive.

"The great wisdom of Mexico about death. The unity of death and life. The passing
of one and the birth of the next one. The eternal circle. And the still greater wisdom of
Mexico: the enjoying of this eternal circle."[98]

83. A couple, colored pencil.

143

84. Three-face mask (1), colored pencil.

85. Three-face mask (2), colored pencil.

145

86. Three-face mask (3), colored pencil.

87. A shot from the Epilogue.
Courtesy of the Museum of Modern Art/Film Stills Archive.

"White skulls are brought into the foreground, and in such an extreme close-up that they become almost tangible.
But the skulls are made of papier-mâché: they are masks of skulls.
Beyond them, in full scale, the merry-go-rounds and the vertical wheels of laughter spin around, flashing into view through the empty eyesockets of the masks, making them wink, as though to say that death is nothing but a hollow carton contraption, through which, all the same, will ever blow the whirlwind of life."[99]

147

88. A shot from the Epilogue.

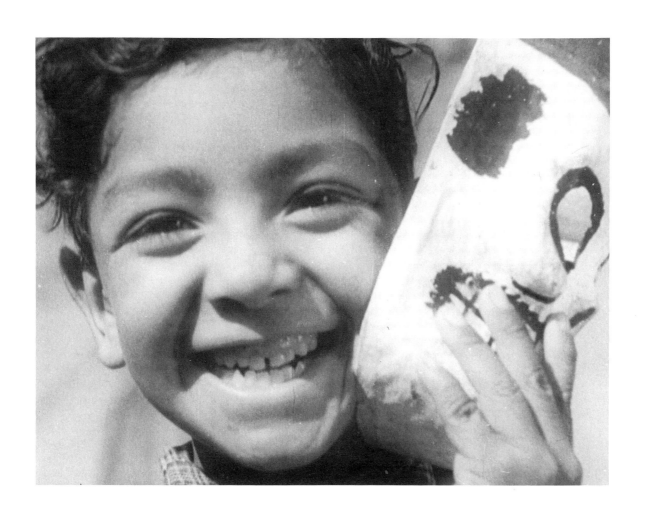

89. A shot from the Epilogue.

90. Eisenstein with a sugar skull, Mexico City.

The following fragments of Eisenstein's writings were taken from different sources:

"The Prometheus of Mexican Painting" (1935), an unfinished essay, was translated into English and published by Jay Leyda in 1982.[100]

"Day of the Dead" (1937) is a passage from Eisenstein's article, *Montage,* which was left unfinished.[101] It was translated for this book by Gaile Sarma.

"Dance Hall in Mexico City" (1941), also translated by Gaile Sarma, is a fragment of an article about an American pilot, Jimmy Collins (1904–36) whom Eisenstein befriended in the USA.[102]

The three fragments "Mexico," "Señor Saldivar," and "Museums at Night" are taken from Eisenstein's *Autobiographical Notes* (1946), the original manuscript of which is in the State Archive of Literature and Art in Moscow.[103] "Señor Saldivar" was translated from Russian for the present book by Gaile Sarma.[104] "Mexico"[105] and "Museums at Night"[106] were taken from *Immoral Memories*[107] (1983), an English translation by Herbert Marshall of *Autobiographical Notes.* A former student of Eisenstein, an English film director and writer, Herbert Marshall appropriated the title from Eisenstein's foreword to his *Autobiographical Notes:* "I must warn you right away: these notes are completely immoral . . . [but it is not] an account of the amorous episodes in the life of a Russian film director. . . . The immorality of these notes will be of quite another kind. They will not moralize . . . nor preach any sermons."[108]

The *Autobiographical Notes,* as well as the other fragments of Eisenstein's writings included in this book, were not published during his life time.

III

REMEMBERING MEXICO

91. *The Mexican Madonna, colored pencil.*

154

MEXICO[109]

During my encounter with Mexico, it seemed to me to be, in all the variety of its contradictions, a sort of outward projection of all those individual lines and features which I carried and carry within me like a tangle of complexes.

Monumental simplicity and unrestrained Baroque (in each of its aspects, Spanish and Aztec). . . . The duality of these attractions finds expression again in my enthusiasm both for the severity of the peon's white costume (a costume that, in both its color and rectilinear silhouette, seems to be the tabula rasa of costumes in general) and for the sculpturesque sequence of gold and silver bas-reliefs, overloaded with gold embroidery, burning on blue, green, orange, and puce satin, that appear under the black hats of the heroic participants of the corridas.

This superabundance was combined with the wealth of capes and black and white lace mantillas of their lady admirers, of tall, Spanish combs, of fans playing and gleaming under the scorching Sunday sun on the stepped tiers around the *Blood and Sand*[110] arenas.

One was as dear to me as the other. I felt as much in harmony with one as with the other. And I delved into the mass of both by means of Eduard Tisse's incomparable camera.

The tropics responded to dreamy sensuality. The intertwining bronze bodies seemed to incarnate the latent rovings of sensuality; here in the over-saturated, overgrown grasping of the lianas, male and female bodies wreathed and intertwined like lianas; they looked in the mirror and saw how the girls of Tehuantepec looked at themselves with black, almond-shaped eyes in the surface of the dreamy tropical creeks, and admired their flowered arrays, reflecting on the golden surface of their bodies. It seemed that embodied in me, and flooded with moonlight, was the rhythmically breathing abundance of the bodies of *esposas de soldados* clasped in the embraces of their husband-soldiers; bodies spread across the whole area of the little eight-sided courtyard of the small fortress guarding the Pacific Ocean port of Acapulco. (Guarding from whom? Unless it be the flights of pelicans, their heads tucked away on one side, plunging like arrows into the amber-colored water of the Gulf.)

The bodies breathe rhythmically and in unison. The very earth itself seems to be breathing, whitened here and there by a veil drawn modestly over a pair among the other bodies, gleaming black in the moonlight, that are not covered by anything. Bodies knowing no shame, bodies to whom what is natural for them is natural, and needs no concealment.

The sergeant and I slowly walk round the narrow parapet, with its narrow loopholes, looking down what appears, from above, to be a battlefield after the bugles have finished sounding the attack, a field of death cast in silver, but is, in fact, a vast cornfield where the seed of countless generations of bronzed children is being sown.

Mexico—lyrical and tender, but also brutal.

It knows the merciless lashes of the whips, lacerating the golden surface of bare skin. The sharp cactus spikes to which, at the height of the civil wars, they tied those already shot half to death, to die in the heat of the desert sands. The sharp spikes that still penetrate the bodies of those who, having made crosses from the cacti's vertical trunks, tie them with rope to their own shoulders, and crawl for hours up to the tops of the pyramids, to glorify the Catholic Madonnas—de Guadalupe, de los Remedios, the Santa Maria Tonantsintl; Catholic Madonnas since Cortes's time, triumphantly occupying the places and positions of the cult of the former pagan gods and goddesses.

In order not to change the age-old routes of the pilgrimages, the crafty monks raised statues and temples to the gods on the very same spots (heights, deserts, pyramids) where the overthrown ancient, heathen gods of the Aztecs, Toltecs, or Mayas had once reigned. To this day streams of pilgrims on religious holidays crawl for hours through the dry dust, tearing skin from their knees, in order to press their parched lips to the heavenly Queen's golden hem or to the fragmented remains of the bones of Her most loyal past disciples (which were obtained for us, from under the altar of the church of San Juan de los Remedios, by the cynical and slightly soiled dean of this church on a pyramid, Father Figueroa, a keen photographer, who went off on his motorcycle every Thursday, without fail, to Mexico City's brothels, situated, for some reason, especially densely around the street bearing the most heroic name from Mexico's past, Guatemotzin). . . . He it was, Guatemotzin, the royal leader with the hawklike, Indian profile, who uttered the famous words "I'm not lying on a bed of roses, either" when the conquering Spaniards, torturing him over fierce braziers, were trying to find out where the wealth and treasure of the land they had enslaved was hidden.

The proud Indian's words were addressed to one of his comrades, who was suffering his share of torture alongside and had dared to utter a groan through clenched teeth.

A bas-relief depicting their heroic sufferings now decorates the pedestal of the monument of Guatemotzin with his head thrown proudly back.

Physical brutality, whether in the "asceticism" of monks' self-flagellation or in the torturing of others, in the blood of the bull or the blood of man, pouring over the sands of countless Sunday corridas every week, after Mass, in a sensual sacrament; the history of unparalleled brutality in crushing the countless uprisings of the peons, who had been driven to a frenzy by the exploitation of the landowners; the retaliatory brutality of the leader of the uprising, Pancho Villa, who ordered prisoners to be hanged naked in order that he and his soldiers might be entertained by the sight of the last physiological reactions of the hanged.

This cruelty of the Mexican does not lie only in bodily mutilation and blood, not only in former slave-owners' favorite treatment of prisoners—top hat on their heads, clothes off, made to perform a frenzied, naked dance in answer to indiscriminate and continuous shooting—but also in that wicked humor, irony, and that special sort of Mexican wit (the features of which are already borne by this ominous tarantella), the so-called vacilada.

92. *Diego Rivera, Frida Kahlo, Sergei Eisenstein, and an unidentified woman in the Riveras' garden in Coyoacan.*
Courtesy of the Lilly Library.

THE PROMETHEUS
OF
MEXICAN PAINTING[111]

Diego is a good, old friend. Across an arc from snowy Moscow, my home, to silent Coyoacan, his home—crowded with huge and prehistoric deities in wood, stone or terra cotta—Aztec and Mayan.

But I have never met the man about whom I am now writing—

 OROZCO.

Our paths crossed three times—in Los Angeles, New York, and Mexico City—and three times we missed the opportunity for the handshake that we have hoped for for so long. Even though geography has not helped us, we managed to find a meeting point. Somewhere in the Elysian fields of ecstasy, we met.

There is an old, convenient method for classifying personalities, especially when two are to be compared: either the Apollonian or the Dionysian. This is so old and convenient that it has gone out of style. Nevertheless, let us adopt it for our pair, Orozco/Diego—Diego/Orozco.

This makes the strangest shape that the eternal wanderers, Apollo and Dionysos, could stumble upon here, in their ceaseless metempsychosis through creative personalities. Really! Imagine swift, slender Apollo recognizing himself in the Pantagruel shape of Gargantua-Diego bursting out of his trousers, wiping his lips after dining à la Grand Gousier on all the greatest walls of Mexico with all the Mexican peoples unrolled on them.

Dionysos, however, would recognize himself at once in the tense, killing, mad glance from behind those thick spectacles recorded by Weston, as thick as the porthole glass of Captain Nemo's *Nautilus*. A Promethean look, and it

159

is not by chance that one of his great frescoes pictures Prometheus. *

Though both difficult *and* ridiculous, this trivial antithesis of Apollo and Dionysos has materialized in its own paradoxical way, in the delirious murals of these two artists.

Brought up within and bursting from the same social explosion, in theme and spirit alike, considered from inside their work is a macrocosm of their two characters, so definite, so opposite, so irreconcilable.

They both plead the same cause.

But next to a Falstaffian Martin Luther shrieks a fiery Savonarola.

As the men—so their work.

Their intensity is distinct. Quantitative in Diego. Qualitative in Orozco.

Square kilometers in area for the one, and so much explosive energy for the other.

Like a magnified self-portrait of the inner Diego—in his gluttony, his voracity of space, sex, food, and form.

The static quality of Diego. Mrs. Bloom of *Ulysses* dashed to the ground in the fresco "Luncheon of the Aesthetes." This is a glove thrown down by Diego to those who are not body and soul with the best there is in Mexico.

Squeezed. Narrowed. Pressed. Concentrated in an outburst of one tremendous, unnatural, clenched, crashing fist—appears Orozco in the Preparatoria walls.

Or he shrinks behind the wall in the endless deserts of the Soldadera's tragic route—seen as through a window opened on a never-to-be-reached horizon.

A scream on a surface *through* form and *through* style. In his "Trench"—three men on a barricade. Only one is balanced on the surface. One flies toward the spectator. Another, following his fist, thrusts himself into the depths beyond the barricade which they are defending. The fist, huge in its proportions, projects from the wall above the heads of those who draw near to look.

The Soldadera walks out across a plain that is twisted by the fierceness of the agave plants. These cutting edges hurt one's eyes as do the pages of *Los de Abajo* ["The Underdogs," a novel by Azuela, illustrated by Orozco]. Walls are not painted in this way. Illustrations are not made like this.

This is not the kind of thing to be painted on walls. On the first floor of the

* In Pomona College, Claremont, California. —J.L.

160

93. José Clemente Orozco, Soldaderas, *lithograph, 1928.*

Preparatoria, while enlarging Posada's satirical print—maidens seeking suitors—who was it who forgot to clear away this chaotic composition, painted in broad strokes as if it were a poster to be seen and then destroyed in a day? It was the same person who, a few steps away, fixed on the wall the story of St. Francis kissing the leper.* You have stumbled into an anatomic catalogue of diseases and deformities.

I saw many a blanching spectator, less in love than I with the beauty that reaches atrocity and the atrocity that can burst into sublime beauty. I saw many a trembling spectator groping for the *cover* of this catalogue, to *close* it,

* Orozco's title for this fresco is "The Friar and the Indio."—J.L.

to escape the fascinating appeal of these pages of horror depicted with all the wounds, the flesh torn by thorns, and the living corruption.

This is the man who plays with the projecting low angles of walls, bringing them together in images of generous hands and poorboxes. Coins, given by the poor, fall into the greasy hands of a priest.

These are not the subjects nor the ways that Orozco should paint on walls. These are not displays of bodies and outlines of machines. The surface explodes. The bodies and columns plunge headlong. An agglomeration of surfaces. Revolutionary force. Cyclone.

Orozco goes on to Dartmouth. There it was the most terrible. Superhuman passions. And amongst these social outcries and fierce caricatures, a handsome young boy, with that ease which only Americans have, sits peacefully reading in that room overflowing with a social tumult of color. Orozco does not compromise. He does not go down to the Stock Exchange in San Francisco like his Apollonian colleague. This must be Mrs. Moody, the tennis champion that Charlie Chaplin and I admired at the Los Angeles tournament, now staring at us from the staircase of the San Francisco Stock Exchange. Does she represent California—or Maternity. Earth. Again Mrs. Bloom?

Have you ever noticed Diego's frescoes in the Upper Gallery of the Educación patio?

Repeated curves of the backs of peasant, soldier, corn and sack, and soldier, corn and sack again?

Where is the optical precedent for this perception?

Is it not in the abundant treelike nopal cactus—the fleshy pancakes of which project themselves in an infinite variety of curves, from circles to straight lines, depending on the angle where they are caught by the spectator's eye, gathered in masses or ranged along . . . walls.

I would dedicate the nopal to Diego.

Myriads of needles flash from it—like the many-walled satires of Diego. His luncheon of the millionaires, of the aesthetes, his burning Indios.

Arriving at an apogee in the tragic buried portrait of Zapata in Chapingo's unforgettable chapel.

But Diego can bloom as well—just as the sharp stings of the nopal, with pink, yellow, blue, and white buds, equal the sweet Sandunga or the flower fiesta of Xochimilco.

94. Diego Rivera, Corn Festival, fresco, Ministry of Agriculture, Mexico City, 1924.

163

Tourists who shudder before his enormous distorted sleeping and waking Earths can repose their nerves as their hearts are quieted in the descent from Mexico City's altitude, down to Cuernavaca—enjoying the linear and coloristic mildness of the "painted" atrocities of the Spanish conquest helpfully embraced by missionary fathers and cheerfully woven in the carpet of the wall . . .

Pitiless to himself, pitiless in what he touches, a hell boiling inside, the man Orozco cannot know such islands of relief.

The iron grill of Cuahtemoc, the pagan martyr, seems ever glowing under him.

The merciless long thorns of the maguey.

Impossible to melt himself into a surface—a triangular wound unable to heal itself—unbending, merciless—I would choose the maguey to characterize Orozco.

Its weapons and its juice—the maddening ritualistic poison of the ancient *pulque*—this is the blood that burns in his veins.

The grin of Quetzalcoatl would be his smile.

Not the smile of conciliating roundness playing over the joyous circles of ironic Mayan masks—Diego's smile!

The portraits that Andrea del Sarto painted of the most varied persons all resemble one person—Andrea himself.

As the painter always flings his emotions upon the walls, why not aspects of himself?

How many self-portraits of Diego smile from the staircase and the gallery walls of the Educación!

These self-portraits may also be symbolic. Inhuman. Superhuman.

The blue covers of Joyce's masterpiece,* the worldwide persecuted *chef-d'oeuvre Ulysses,* become the frame for another portrait of Diego. Symbolic this time—but not by his brush. This time by a pen, perhaps surpassing him in vigor . . .

Once more take an hour's stroll through the galleries of Educación. Suddenly Diego's frescoes melt together, growing identical, incessantly

---

* From the enthusiastic early draft: "*Ulysses*—Joyce's masterpiece—the greatest work in world literature, overshadowing Rabelais, Balzac, Dante . . ."—J.L.

164

flowing—no commas, no stops—resembling that last chapter of *Ulysses,* the inner monologue of Mrs. Leopold Bloom.

Diego flows across these walls in one gorgeous multicolored stream, not destroying like lava, but like mysterious Nature in periods of springtime and fertilization, vitality overflowing from one shape into another, ever reemerging in an infinite diversity of forms and creations.

Mrs. Bloom is more than a singer and the occasional wife of an advertising agent. More—Mrs. Bloom is the Mother of Things. Mother Earth. And her perpetual fertility—she is the mightiest personification of this fundamental principle among the symbols of world literature.

I would set up Diego alongside Mother Earth and Mother of Things, with his arched exodus of animals in human shape—human beings reduced to the exploitation of animals.

The womb could be the symbol of the continuing creativeness of this man. . . .

We love that in which we recognize ourselves . . .

As for myself I love both emotionally through myself—this concerns the single road of knowledge.

It is between these two poles that I shuttle back and forth.

Let me try a quick outline of the polarity of these two great masters.

I offer an original response by finding the same polarity at the core of myself and of my cinema—of my moving frescoes (for we also work on walls!).

Potemkin bursts through the screen into the auditorium.

The General Line pulls onto the plane of contemplative space both the vertical

    and

the horizontal—

such is the definition given me by Fernand Leger (see *Le Monde*).

This is what gives me the possibility of seeing their work *in this way.*

This is what forces me to see them *in this way.*

Perhaps it's a vision, a prevision.

Is a synthesis possible on a wall's space?

Can it contain the furious tension that pulls across its surface like a bow about to let fly its arrow, like a balloon about to burst—can all this be put on a wall?—and still be a wall?

Near the large official patio of the Preparatoria where tourists are accustomed to stroll, there is a smaller patio.*

Impossible *not* to see Diego's frescoes in the Secretariat.

But it is only with great tolerance that you are shown Orozco's frescoes.

And it is only by being stubborn that you can persuade the guides to lead you to the little patio behind the School.

To the sound of whispers, the malicious sniffing of aged professors—aesthetes who acquired their concepts of art from those who taught them . . .

It is here, amidst these scratched and mutilated walls and fading colors, that one perceives, nearly lost beneath the wall's surface, luminous next to bald white plaster, unfinished and empty,—

a coffin of intense aquamarine.

We know this treatment of coffins from the engravings of Posada.

Our screen knows something similar.

The mourning brown faces of workers burying a comrade, this coffin stretches through the surface in a tragic crack in the silent conflict between pain and anger . . .

The conflict on the wall is a paroxysm of despair, wanting to burst into sobs—

—and frozen in a synthesis of the wall.

The fresco is unfinished.

Other frescoes have not followed it.

A prison-door was slammed shut behind the author . . .

Siqueiros.

(and the embryo of this fresco's synthesis has no continuation).

The lid of the blue coffin is closed again.

A prison-cell lends itself badly to fresco. Little gray paintings—sobs crucified on the easel—their format limited by cot and stool. Their color comes from the close-stool. Gray-brown paintings in the semi-obscurity of incarceration—the fatal rhythm of detention followed the procession behind the blue coffin.

Prison molded David Alfaro {Siqueiros} into a painter.

Synthesis is a dangerous thing . . . It sometimes descends from the wall,

* This section of Eisenstein's notes is concerned with Siqueiros, whose described "Burial of a Worker" (eventually destroyed) governed part of the Prologue to *Que Viva Mexico!*—J.L.

to use the picturesque amidst the melée as a substitute for painting a penetration into the melée of reality.

Gray paintings in which the deep somber eyes of Indios endlessly question; similar to the gray shadows of memory, they inhabit the great empty room that is perched high on a rock raised over Taxco (there's a dizzying balcony without a guard-rail) where Siqueiros now works, preparing an exhibition for New York, that New York of dealers and wealthy patrons.

In the blinding sunlight, choking the red of the flowers that they call *sangre del toro*—Taxco seems not to exist.

Attentive shutters protect the gray-blue eyes that are used to the semi-darkness of the prison-cell. Hiding the movements of the brush that used to be a gun, and at any moment may become one again.

Farther down, countless churches, countless chapels reflect the heat from roofs of Spanish tiles . . .

And the two opposing lines continue to burn on the walls of the world—even beyond the borders of Mexico . . .

[unfinished]

1935

95. *A Mexican, colored pencil.*

168

DANCE HALL
IN MEXICO CITY[112]

Mexico City . . .

Right now we are both at the entrance to the dance hall.

Around us are bronze men in blue outfits, checked and striped shirts. Some have their sombreros on their heads, some in their hands (so as not to muss the part, which seems like a ravine, cleverly cut through the mass of black, coarse, unbending hair).

Cheap rings worn on labor-hardened fingers wink with false brilliance at the equally cheap earrings in the ears of bronze girls.

Their powder—and the lilac shade which it lends to bronze skin—seems in the blue and red neon light like a sore on the cheeks.

Rouge—like black gaps.

That's how, in his youth, the amazing José Clemente Orozco drew prostitutes on the walls of "pulquerias," cheap Mexican taverns.

That's how they gaze out from the black and white prints of the teacher of young Mexican artists, the incomparable José Guadalupe Posada.

The eyes of these "muchachas" burn feverishly.

The gleaming material shines, tightly wrapping their resilient bodies.

Inside, "Danson" is going on.

And greedily listening at the door to the music and scuffling of dancing feet are those of their "caballeros" who don't have ten "centavos" to buy a ticket and the accompanying snapshot of a naked girl, and rush into the three dance halls connected by archways.

Actually, these archways don't connect the halls, they divide them.

And although passage from one to the other and to the third in descending order is permitted, there is no return passage.

In the halls there are various prices, and a paltry difference in price divides the dancers, like iron bars.

Collins and I move through the first two halls into the third.

I feel like Virgil, leading Dante through the circles of hell.

Bosch, Goya, Dix, and Grosz all pale before this bacchanal of lepers.

The light here is dimmer.

The music—from a distance—is fainter. The "Danson" is under way, that amazing dance, in which from time to time, in the midst of the most sharp motion, a couple suddenly, for several beats, freezes completely motionless, facing one another, and stands as if rooted, until they again continue the tormenting sensuality, or the quick tempo of rhythmic body movements.

Just as motionlessly, their bodies barely touching, they stand—long and longingly—in the dark streets, under each tree, along the endless walls of the city hospital or in the side alleys of the "alameda"—the city park. Here they stand still in the dance.

At such moments, the dance hall is frightening: it seems like a stiffened corpse, still trembling inside to the beat of the orchestra's screaming rhythm.

In the semidarkness, the figures come to life and float away. . . .

Drooping paper flowers, white teeth splitting dark faces with a smile. A black eye. A naked shoulder—all black and blue. A neck covered with bite marks. A blood-red bruise.

In the corner is a strange old man. He is drawing with a thin India-ink brush, on the shirt of a "caballero," the initials of his lady, over the spot where his blazing heart is beating.

The brush tickles. All around him, they're cracking jokes.

But the bronze "caballero" is afraid to move; it's his only shirt and he can't mess up the drawing.

All around there is raucous laughter.

They're dancing.

But not everyone is whirling around. Most stay motionless. Most of them are on the benches. And most of them are sleeping.

The explanation is simple:
The third dance hall is cheaper than a dosshouse.

And to the scrape of the orchestra, to the rhythmic shaking of the floor from the rhythmically shaking dancers, on the benches all around, dozens of homeless, unemployed, and hopeless people are sleeping.

(Translated by Gaile Sarma)

96. His Excellency, pen and ink.

172

SEÑOR SALDIVAR [113]

. . . An old man . . . almost incoherently muttering, although, as before, he sits in state at the head of a long table in the dining hall of the impoverished hacienda Tetlapayac. . . .

The eyes of the old Señor Saldivar, eternally polite and amiable, light up only at the sight of food and drink.

However, the old man is not quite bereft of strength, and even curiosity.

The manager, Señor Nicolas from Santander in Spain. . . . The boundless fields of maguey are ornamented here and there with little crosses. . . . The crosses mark the tracks of the strict discipline of Señor Nicolas.

Señor Nicolas recently bought a Packard.

In a week, the Packard was wrecked and removed from service.

Señor Nicolas cannot break the habit of treating the Packard like an unbroken mustang.

The Packard flies through the ravines, like a horse.

The Packard's relationship with the man from Santander was ended by a powerful bull.

The bull saw the Packard not as a horse, but as a member of his own tribe.

The powerful horns of the Andalusian beauty bent the radiator of his unwelcome rival.

The Packard lies on its side.

At filming locations we are often visited by a strange procession.

Two striped charros ahead.

High on a horse, under an umbrella, the ancient Señor Saldivar.

173

And his personal servant, the "mozo" Mattias, in the rear. . . .

At night the scenes are different.

The old man calls Mattias to his lofty bedroom.

The old man is holding a gun in his hands and sobbing.

He asks Nicolas to shoot him.

He is ruining his grandson.

He is destroying the hacienda.

Nicolas and Mattias forcibly place the unstable old gentleman in bed.

And in the morning he looks just as lasciviously on the green peppers stuffed with pomegranates and nuts, and other exotic viands, which the lanky and bemoustached Guadalupe places before him.

The next morning, the girl who plays the lord's daughter in the picture rushes indignantly to me—it seems that the evening before this half-mummified old man had made her a most direct proposition, and offered to drive off with her to the city.

This is a lot nearer to what we know about the old man with false teeth, in the strange old woman's cap that shaded him from the sun as he rode through the fields on horseback.

He squandered money without restraint in Paris.

He was always losing money at the races.

He never crawled out of his dress-coat and white tie, turning night to day and day to night in the golden places of Paris.

It's hard to believe. Now he's a ruin.

But now, the ancient Señor Saldivar shows us a particular honor.

He goes for several days to Mexico City and invites us to his place.

Oyster soup, prepared in a silver saucepan.

Fish such as the world has never seen.

Lobsters.

The rest of the dinner is lost in a certain cloudy confusion.

The combination of Parisian refinement with the carnivorousness of the New World is as if broad Chapultepec Avenue joined the Bois de Boulogne with the growth of the tropics, or as [if] the soaring iron architecture from the age of Napoleon III and Maximilian entwined itself with the bronze faces and blue overalls of the modern inhabitants of Mexico City.

The old man is transformed.

And if he isn't wearing a dress-coat, but rather some senile house-coat, all the same, by the movement of his hands, however much they have lost their strength, by his smile, which has overcome the flabbiness of his drooping lips, by his sparkling wit, so unexpectedly breaking loose from his almost incoherent muttering, one could resurrect the image of that formerly brilliant social lion, probably just as mysterious and extravagant as the rather improbable Brazilians in Balzac's novels.

(Translated by Gaile Sarma)

97. A dancer, colored pencil.

DAY OF THE DEAD[114]

The ironic attitude toward death completely permeates a second, life-affirming aspect of the festival Day of the Dead.

The first is devoted to memories of the deceased, prayers for them, their unseen presence among the living—for them the table is set, for them food is spread out on the graves, among the forest of candles burning all night in the mountain cemetery . . . or on the shore of Lake Patscuaro in the state of Michoacan. But from the first light of dawn, life begins to claim its own; life is for the living. And recalling the amusing sign of the cafe opposite the main entrance to the famous Parisian cemetery Père Lachaise "Au repos des vivants" ("place of rest for . . . the living"), life asserts its rights. Food and drink are gulped down, fireworks are set off (in broad daylight!) alternating with more traditional expressions of joy—pistols are fired, carrousels revolve, shops and booths do business, and on the graves of the cemetery, among the burnt-out candles and the crepe-shrouded portraits of the deceased brought from home, they are diligently involved in the propagation of humankind.

Food and enjoyment on that day all carry the emblem of death. The pitchers are skulls. The sweets are skulls. There are especially large, decorated sugar skulls, the size of a child's head, and bearing the name of a departed loved one on the forehead. Little chocolate coffins compete with the sugar-made deceased. And by the end of the day, all of that is dissolved in the stomachs of little bronze children, from their tender years accustomed to associate the skull with sugar, and not with the gloomy Franciscan slogan, the traditional skull decorated with crossed bones: "I was you—you will be me."

In the last sequence of the film, a chubby boy was breaking a sugar skull bigger than his head, and devouring its remains with relish! But not only the sweets—a sea of toys decorated with skeletons, skulls and coffins flood the bazaars on those days, taking over the "alamedas" (squares). Sheets and leaflets with ironic songs and political pamphlets (epitaphs for living political figures, supposedly "at rest with God") and the matchless prints of the incomparable Posada, always on the same ironic theme of death, are passed from reader to reader, adults and children, their faces concealed in the dance by masks . . . of the same death. In their buttonholes are again emblems of death, but with social attributes: a skull in a top-hat, a skull in the broad-brimmed hat of a hacendado. A skull in a matador's cap, with a braid on the bone of a neck. A skull in the three-cornered hat of a minister, the helmet of a fireman, the service cap of a gendarme. There is a skull under a general's kepi, and a skull in a bishop's tiara.

This is Mexican defiance of death, an affirmation of the vitality of life.

(Translated by Gaile Sarma)

*98. Eisenstein at the National Museum of Anthropology, Mexico City.
Courtesy of the Lilly Library.*

MUSEUMS AT NIGHT[115]

In Chichen Itza . . . the curator of the Museum of Ancient Mayan Culture decided to take me through the museum's halls at night. . . .

The nights there are pitch black and tropical. Even the Southern Cross, which shamefacedly pokes only its little end above the Mexican horizon, does not light them up.

But in the museum the electricity went off at the very moment we crossed the threshold of the treasured "secret department" of the museum, where the revelry of the ancient Mayas' sensual imagination is carved in stone.

The statues also gained in weirdness, absurdity, disproportion, and scale, because they were suddenly snatched out of the darkness by matches struck now here, now there.

Tolstoy, in *Childhood*—or is it in *Adolescence?*—describes the effect of lightning flashes illuminating galloping horses.

So instantaneous were the flashes that each succeeded in capturing only one phase of the horses' movement.

The horses seemed motionless. . . .

The unexpected striking of the matches in the different parts of this hall, filled with motionless stone monsters, made these monsters, on the contrary, seem as though they had come to life.

From the change of direction of the light in the intervals before the matches burned out, it seemed as if, during the periods of darkness, the monsters had managed to change position and place in order to gape with their wide, round, bulging, dead, granite eyes from a new viewpoint at those who were disturbing their age-old peace.

However . . . the majority of these stone monsters, rearing out of the dark, had no eyes at all.

But two barrel-shaped roundish gods, in particular, had eyes. I was led to them through the stone reefs of the others (which were in the main ellipsoidal) by the hospitable match of the curator of these precious remains of antiquity.

Light and dark interrupted each other.

Interwove.

Followed each other in turn.

But the speech of my Virgil, who was conducting me through this dark circled Purgatory of mankind's early notions, came pouring out, uninterrupted. Facts and more facts about the history of the belief in gods endowed with "double strength" eddied unceasingly through this interplay of light and dark. The interplay of light and dark itself began to seem an intertwining of the light of reason with the dark depths of man's psyche.

Two globe-shaped granite gods who had this absolute strength faced me with a welcoming smile.

Why two of them?

Each of them was built so that he (or she) had no need at all of his (or her) partner.

One could be sure of this only by touching.

And not just because it was dark in the hall.

But because the object of the investigation was secreted deep under the globes of their bellies.

"Don't be afraid to touch," my guide told me. "Touching it was and still is considered to have curative value and to give the toucher great strength. Feel how much the granite has been worn away. . . ."

And I recalled the famous statue of Peter in the cathedral named after him in Rome.

The leg half kissed away by those who fervently pressed their lips to it.

Here the matter was simpler and clearer.

To touch these statues of gods, though a symbolic action, is to join them.

By touching their "double strength," you yourself acquire a part of that superhuman strength.

The miraculous strength proves itself.

Suddenly the electricity comes on, and we spend the last part of our pilgrimage to the gods, with their internal contradictions, in the yellowish electric light.

NOTES AND REFERENCES

1. Jay Leyda, ed., *Eisenstein 2: A Premature Celebration of Eisenstein's Centenary* (Calcutta: Seagull Books, 1985), p. 47. Letter to Ester Shub.

2. Harry Geduld and Ronald Gottesman, eds., *Sergei Eisenstein and Upton Sinclair: The Making and Unmaking of Que Viva Mexico!* (Bloomington: Indiana University Press, 1970), pp. 281–82. Eisenstein's letter to Salka Viertel, written on January 27, 1932.

3. The remaining portions of the footage, many years later, were carefully gathered into an educational film by Jay Leyda, a former student of Eisenstein and the first translator of Eisenstein's writings from Russian into English.

4. Quoted in Inga Karetnikova, *Eisenstein's Mexican Drawings* (Rome: Beniamino Carucci Pub. 1973), p. 12.

5. Sergei Eisenstein, *Immoral Memories: An Autobiography,* trans. Herbert Marshall (Boston: Houghton Mifflin Company, 1983), p. 181.

6. Sergei Eisenstein, *Film Form* (New York: Harcourt, Brace & World, 1969), p. 6.

7. Jack London, "The Mexican" in *Best Short Stories* (Doubleday & Co., 1945), p. 226.

8. Vladimir Mayakovsky, "I, Myself" in *Mayakovsky,* trans. Herbert Marshall (London: Dennis Dobson, 1965), p. 88.

9. The director's father, Mikhail Eisenstein, a successful architect in Riga, held the rank of state councillor; his mother, Julia, was the only heiress of her wealthy father, an industrialist in St. Petersburg.

10. French writer and film historian Leon Moussinac, who visited Moscow in November of 1927, wrote about the Russian director:

To be in the presence of Eisenstein was to be in the presence of genius.

The intensity of this presence, which I felt from the first moment of our first meeting in November, 1927, overwhelmed me. It was impossible to escape, it was both physical and intellectual. Physical because of the mobility of his face and hands, the strength of the shoulders on which the powerful form of his head was set, the energy and intelligence radiating from his whole person. . . .

. . . He possessed a great store of knowledge which he used without affectation. I could see that he was gifted with extraordinary powers of invention and discovery, that he had a deep passion for innovation and creation.

Leon Moussinac, *Sergei Eisenstein* (New York: Crown Publishers, 1970), p. 21.

11. Bertram D. Wolfe, *Diego Rivera, His Life and Times* (Robert Hale Limited, 1939), p. 242.

12. Some lines in Mayakovsky's Mexican poems sound very "Eisensteinian": "Years and centuries / you have cut down / the bowed heads of days / still the weathered stones of Mexico City / whisper the past to me." Vladimir Mayakovsky, *Complete Works in Twelve Volumes* (Moscow: Khudozhestvennaya Literatura, 1939), v. 7., p. 134 (in Russian).

13. Vladimir Mayakovsky, "My Discovery of America," *Complete Works in Twelve Volumes*, v. 7, p. 328.

14. Ibid., v. 2, p. 36.

15. Hayden Herrera, *Frida: A Biography of Frida Kahlo* (New York: Harper & Row, 1983), p. 102.

16. Sergei Eisenstein, *Immoral Memories*, p. 194.

17. Quoted in Jay Leyda and Zina Voynow, *Eisenstein at Work* (New York: Pantheon Books/The Museum of Modern Art, 1982), p. 58.

18. Ivor Montagu, *With Eisenstein in Hollywood* (New York: International Publishers, 1967), p. 141.

19. Harry Geduld and Ronald Gottesman, *Eisenstein and Sinclair*, p. 16.

20. The details of the relationship between Eisenstein and the Sinclairs are documented in Geduld and Gottesman, *Eisenstein and Sinclair*.

21. Eisenstein's unfamiliarity with the financial aspect of film production can be illustrated with a story Ivor Montagu told: In Hollywood there was a bookseller who in his youth fought with [Pancho] Villa. Eisenstein regularly visited his bookstore. Once Eisenstein asked him: "How much would it cost to make a reasonably economical film in Mexico? Mostly documentary, no professional actors—could it be done for—say—twenty-five thousand dollars?" The bookseller . . . replied: "Possibly," and this information, thus obtained, Eisenstein optimistically relayed to Sinclair. . . .

Ivor Montagu, *With Eisenstein in Hollywood*, p. 131.

22. Harry Geduld and Ronald Gottesman, Eisenstein and Sinclair, p. 30.

23. Ibid., p. 44.

24. Rostislav Yurenev, *Sergei Eisenstein,* Part Two (Moscow: Iskusstvo, 1988), p. 38 (in Russian).

25. Sergei Eisenstein, *Immoral Memories,* p. 211.

26. Anita Brenner, *Idols Behind Altars* (New York: Payson & Clarke, 1929), p. 62.

27. *Typage*—the term used by Eisenstein to define specific social types in his films—soldier, worker, capitalist, and so forth, usually played by nonprofessional performers whose appearance was best suited for their types. A *typage* is easily identified by the audience.

28. Sergei Eisenstein, *Film Essays and a Lecture,* edited by Jay Leyda (Princeton: Princeton University Press, 1982), p. 230.

29. Sergei Eisenstein, *Immoral Memories,* p. 212.

30. Quoted in Inga Karetnikova, *Eisenstein's Mexican Drawings,* p. 87.

31. Octavio Paz, *Alternating Current* (New York: Viking Press, 1973), p. 108.

32. Sergei Eisenstein, *Selected Works in Six Volumes* (Moscow: Iskusstvo, 1964), p. 264 (in Russian).

33. Sergei Eisenstein, *Immoral Memories,* p. 34.

34. Marie Seton, *Sergei M. Eisenstein: A Biography* (London: Dennis Dobson, 1978), p. 216.

35. The Mexican drawings that Eisenstein brought back to Moscow, along with his personal papers, were filed away, after his death in 1948, in the Central Archives in Moscow. Only in the late 1960s was I able to publish, in Moscow, about a hundred of his drawings with the publishing house Soviet Artist. The majority of them had never been published before. With some alterations the Italian edition of the Mexican drawings came out in Rome in 1973, published by Beniamino Carucci.

36. Quoted in Inga Karetnikova, *Eisenstein's Mexican Drawings,* p. 13.

37. Harry Geduld and Ronald Gottesman, *Eisenstein and Sinclair,* p. 67.

38. Sergei Eisenstein, *Immoral Memories,* p. 4.

39. Leon Moussinac, *Sergei Eisenstein,* p. 128.

40. Sergei Eisenstein, *Immoral Memories,* p. 260.

41. Quoted in Inga Karetnikova, *Eisenstein's Mexican Drawings,* p. 131.

42. Harry Geduld and Ronald Gottesman, *Eisenstein and Sinclair,* p. 149.

43. Sergei Eisenstein, *Selected Works in Six Volumes,* v. 1, p. 150.

44. Marie Seton, *Sergei M. Eisenstein: A Biography,* p. 195.

45. Sergei Eisenstein, *Selected Works in Six Volumes,* v. 1, p. 462.

46. *Oprichnina:* this Russian word has several meanings. Here it means the private army of Ivan the Terrible, his security police notorious for its cruelty and gang tactics.

47. Sergei Eisenstein, *Selected Works in Six Volumes*, v. 1, p. 46.

48. Sergei Eisenstein, *Film Essays and a Lecture*, p. 225.

49. Harry Geduld and Ronald Gottesman, *Eisenstein and Sinclair*, p. 182.

50. Ibid., p. 212.

51. Sergei Eisenstein, *Immoral Memories*, p. 211.

52. In 1959, on one of his visits to Moscow, Siqueiros told me that in all his life no one else had impressed him as much as Eisenstein with his personality, as intriguing as a work of art and possessing the same unexpected "montage" as his films.

53. Sergei Eisenstein, *Immoral Memories*, p. 37.

54. Ibid.

55. Sergei Eisenstein, *Nonindifferent Nature*, trans. by Herbert Marshall (Cambridge: Cambridge University Press, 1987), p. 363.

56. Harry Geduld and Ronald Gottesman, *Eisenstein and Sinclair*, p. 285.

57. Sergei Eisenstein, *Nonindifferent Nature*, p. 382.

58. Harry Geduld and Ronald Gottesman, *Eisenstein and Sinclair*, p. 49.

59. Sergei Eisenstein, *Selected Works in Six Volumes*, v. 2, p. 362.

60. Harry Geduld and Ronald Gottesman, *Eisenstein and Sinclair*, p. 281.

61. Quoted in Inga Karetnikova, *Eisenstein's Mexican Drawings*, p. 12.

62. Aldolfo Best-Mangard, "Mexico into Cinema," *Theatre Arts Monthly* (November 1932): 926.

63. Jay Leyda, *Eisenstein 2*, v. 2, p. 30.

64. Sergei Eisenstein, *Selected Works in Six Volumes*, v. 1, p. 153.

65. Jay Leyda, "Eisenstein's notes for the epilogue of *Que Viva Mexico!*," *Sight & Sound*, 6 (1958): 306.

66. The well-known constructivist Rodchenko, who was close to Eisenstein, wrote in his diary, "On my *dacha* in Pushkino I walk about and look at nature: here a bush, there a tree, over here a ditch, a gully. . . . Everything is accidental and unorganized. Nothing even to put in a photograph. It's not interesting. Only these pine trees are passable—tall, naked, almost telephone poles. . . ."

67. Marie Seton, *Sergei M. Eisenstein: A Biography*, p. 214.

68. Sergei Eisenstein, *Selected Works in Six Volumes*, v. 1, pp. 203–540.

69. thèse (Fr)—thesis.

70. Sergei Eisenstein, *Immoral Memories*, p. 2.

71. Ibid.

72. Ibid., p. 178.

73. Ibid., pp. 58–59.

74. Sergei Eisenstein, *Selected Works in Six Volumes*, v. 1, p. 397.

75. Sergei Eisenstein, *Que Viva Mexico!* (New York, Arno Press, 1972). Reprint

of the 1951 edition published by Vision, London.

76. Sergei Eisenstein, *The Film Sense* (New York: Harcourt, Brace, Jovanovich, 1969), p. 251.

77. Sergei Eisenstein, *Que Viva Mexico!,* Prologue.

78. Sergei Eisenstein, *Immoral Memories*, p. 211.

79. Sergei Eisenstein, *Selected Works in Six Volumes,* v. 3, p. 175.

80. Ibid., v. 1, p. 265.

81. Sergei Eisenstein, *Immoral Memories*, p. 34.

82. Sergei Eisenstein, quoted in Inga Karetnikova, *Eisenstein's Mexican Drawings,* p. 13.

83. Jay Leyda, *Eisenstein, 2,* p. 28 (from a letter to the poet Victoria Ocampo).

84. Sergei Eisenstein, *Immoral Memories*, p. 5.

85. Sergei Eisenstein, *Selected Works in Six Volumes,* v. 1, p. 462.

86. Sergei Eisenstein, quoted in Marie Seton, *Sergei M. Eisenstein: A Biography,* p. 197.

87. Sergei Eisenstein, *Selected Works in Six Volumes,* v. 1, p. 265.

88. Ibid., v. 4, p. 638.

89. Sergei Eisenstein, *Nonindifferent Nature,* p. 381.

90. Sergei Eisenstein, *Selected Works in Six Volumes,* v. 1, p. 504.

91. Ibid., v. 3, p. 445.

92. Ibid., v. 5, p. 434.

93. Sergei Eisenstein, *Nonindifferent Nature,* p. 362.

94. Salka Viertel, *The Kindness of Strangers* (New York: Holt, Rinehart and Winston, 1969), p. 154.

95. Harry Geduld and Ronald Gottesman, *Eisenstein and Sinclair,* pp. 280–82 (Eisenstein always wrote Salka's name with a Z).

96. Salka Viertel, *The Kindness of Strangers,* p. 159.

97. Ibid.

98. Mary Seton, *Sergei M. Eisenstein: A Biography,* p. 19.

99. Sergei Eisenstein, *Immoral Memories,* pp. 220–30.

100. In Sergei Eisenstein, *Film Essays and Lecture,* pp. 222–31.

101. Sergei Eisenstein, *Selected Works in Six Volumes,* v. 2, p. 365.

102. Ibid., v. 5, pp. 447–49.

103. Ibid., v. 1, pp. 210–550.

104. Ibid., pp. 461–63.

105. Sergei Eisenstein, *Immoral Memories,* pp. 181–83.

106. Ibid., pp. 178–79.

107. Ibid.

108. Ibid., p. 1.

109. From Sergei Eisenstein, *Immoral Memories,* pp. 181–83.

110. A novel about bullfighting, *Blood and Sand,* by Vicente Blasco-Ibáñez (1867–1928).

111. From Sergei Eisenstein, *Film Essays and Lecture,* pp. 222–31.

112. Sergei Eisenstein, *Selected Works in Six Volumes,* v. 5, pp. 447–49.

113. Ibid., v. 1, pp. 461–63.

114. Ibid., v. 2, p. 365.

115. Sergei Eisenstein, *Immoral Memories,* pp. 178–79.

LIST OF ILLUSTRATIONS

INDEX

About the Authors

Inga Karetnikova, a former Guggenheim, Carnegie-Mellon, and Radcliffe Institute Fellow, has lectured and conducted numerous workshops on film and art in many colleges and universities across the United States. Author of *Eisenstein's Mexican Drawings* and a book on screen writing, *How Scripts are Made,* she teaches at Boston University and lives in Cambridge, Massachusetts.

Leon Steinmetz, artist and author, has had shows of his art in Rome, London, and New York, and has taught creative writing at Harvard.

MEXICO ACCORDING TO EISENSTEIN

Edited by Dana Asbury
Designed by Milenda Nan Ok Lee
Typography in Garamond and Epitaph
by Keystone Typesetting, Inc.
Printed by Thomson-Shore, Inc.
Printed in the U.S.A.